REAR ADMIRAL (RS) LAURIO H. DESTEFANI

THE MALVINAS, THE SOUTH GEORGIAS AND THE SOUTH SANDWICH ISLANDS, the conflict with Britain

Corvettes "Descubierta" and "Atrevida". Malaspina expedition (1789 - 1794). Watercolour by E. Biggeri.

EDIPRESS S.A.
Sgo. del Estero 286 - 6th floor - Ap. 1
Buenos Aires - Argentina

**Rear Admiral (retired, in service)
Laurio H. Destéfani**

Head of the Department of Naval Historical Studies of the Argentine Navy.

Graduate in History (University of Buenos Aires).

Member and Secretary of the National Academy of History.

Doctor (Honoris Causa) of the San Juan Bosco University of Comodoro Rivadavia.

Member of the Comisión Nacional de la Reconquista y Defensa de Buenos Aires.

President of the Brownian Institute.

Rising the argentine flag on the Malvinas Islands (at Puerto Soledad), on 6th November 1820. Oil painting by Emilio Biggeri.

INTRODUCTION

The publication of this book was totally paid for with the contributions made by the private companies and state enterprises which are mentioned above. Edipress S.A., a company in the field of journalism and publishing, conceived the idea of printing a book in Spanish, English, French, German, Portuguese and Italian and distributing it throughout the world to fulfill a need to clarify the Argentine truth and make it known everywhere.

Thus it may be possible for people who do not have access to more material on the subject of our Malvinas, and especially in the case of those abroad, to better understand how substantial our rights are.

The simple geographical, historical and legal truths, without any exaggeration, constitute the best defence of our rights of sovereignty over the three Southern archipelagos and the Cormoran and Negra rocks (the Auroras).

As this book is being finished, the fighting still continues and the peace talks do not seem to be successful; but this is the moment to re-temper our spirit, because whatever the cost may be and hewever long it may take, the three archipelagos must be ours, because our cause is just.

To all those who contributed with their work, especially to the staff of the Department of Naval Historical Sudies, my grateful thanks.

Buenos Aires, May 24th, 1982.

LAURIO H. DESTEFANI
Rear Admiral (retired, in service)

THE MALVINAS ARE ARGENTINE

For historical reasons, because they were Spanish until 1811 and consequently Argentine by inheritance until 1833, when they were usurped by Great Britain in a time of peace and friendship with our country.

For geographical reasons, because they lie within the Argentine continental shelf, only 346 kilometres away, whereas they are 12,000 kilometres from England.

For reasons of international law, as from Tordesillas and successive treaties through to Nootka Sound—1790, they were always Spanish and Argentina inherited them, occupied them and exercised sovereignty over them.

The South Georgias and the South Sandwich islands are Argentine through their geographical location, their proximity and also based on historical facts of sovereignty.

And lastly because, from 1833 onwards, which was the year in which we were attacked, we have never given them up, nor will we ever do so!

**DEDICATED TO DRS. RICARDO CAILLET BOIS AND
ERNESTO J. FITTE, WHO WERE UNFORGETTABLE
TEACHERS AND FRIENDS.**

CHAPTER I

British Imperialism

When, on the 2nd of ~~August~~ April 1982, Argentina recovered the Malvinas and the South Georgia Islands, she reaffirmed her rights over the three southern archipelagos (including the Sandwich Islands). Thus a war continued which was started by England when, on the 3rd of January 1833, she usurped the Malvinas at a time when full peace reigned, since the Treaty of Friendship, Trade and Navigation of 1825 between both countries was in full force. There is no doubt, then, that the Argentine actions undertaken on the 2nd of April 1982, were the response to this usurpation, after a century and a half of patient negotiations without any results.

All it takes is to study a map,, look at the Atlantic Ocean, and find the Islands, to fully understand that, geographically, the three southern archipelagos involved in the controversy can only belong to Argentina; but the knowledge of the solid historic events, those that cannot be denied even when discussed in detail, is fundamental to establish that the sovereignty of those archipelagos belongs exclusively to Argentina.

When the British occupation of the islands took place, Argentina had just finished waging two transcendental wars; the War of Independence and the War with Brazil, and she was engaged in an arduous internal controversy to establish her political and institutional future.

Through the War of Independence, Argentina not only obtained her freedom from Spain, but she also freed Chile and Peru, and she also participated in the obtention of the independence of Ecuador. Moreover she did not establish political or commercial links with the liberated nations, but rather left them completely free, in spite of the price paid with the blood of her men. In this respect, San Martin's achievement is exemplary and is rarely paralleled in world history.

Then this Nation, which had been freeing other nations, found herself involved in the defence of what always had been her own territory, and had to wage a war against the Brazilian Empire, thus depleting her small available naval power.

The Civil War was the result of different ideas on how to organize the country, all of which were valid, but which produced a situation of internal weakness.

It was precisely at this moment, when Argentina was wounded and disorganized, that Great Britain availed herself of the action undertaken by an American ship so as to take something away from a country she was good friends with, and a trading partner of, since England had great strength as she ruled supreme over the oceans.

Must we believe that the countries of the Northern Hemisphere are unaware of these events? Or that commercial or economic interests are of more importance to them than justice?

Seldom has Argentina acted with such unanimity adopting measures as hard as in this case, in which she continues a fight she did not bring about and which, we repeat, started in 1833.

To quote but one example, nothing similar happened when Czechoslovakia or Hungary were taken over.

In this war a major battle is being fought, the battle for recognition and appreciation by the world of everything that law and freedom represent versus materialistic bowing to force or convenience.

This is a struggle which goes far back into time, really it is the basic struggle of man. If law, justice and freedom triumph, man will be closer to perfection and to God; otherwise man will fall back to "law of the jungle" levels, which were already abandoned in prehistoric days.

Towards the middle of the XVIth Century, Spain was the foremost nation of the world and dominated the seas with her fleets of warships and her vessels of discovery as well as having her ships bring back the treasures from America. It was then that a new idea was conceived, new in concept and new in concretion.

Until modern times, the large empires had been the result of clashes in which the more powerful civilized nations took part with their armies, sometimes supported by their navies and thus conquered the lands of the nations they defeated and so increased the size of their domains. This is what happened in the cases of the Egyptian, the Assyrian, the Macedonian and the Roman Empires.

The Spanish Empire was based on the conquest of America, where kingdoms and tribes enjoyed a certain degree of civilization but were not strong at sea. What was different was that America was far removed from Europe and all the Spanish power had to be moved across the ocean.

The British Empire expanded in America, in Asia, in Oceania and in Africa. These locations were also far away and separated by vast oceans and to consolidate her Empire, England considered it necessary to "rule the waves", that is, to have absolute naval supremacy. The peak period for the establishment of this Empire was during the XIXth Century and its decline started with the loss of this absolute supremacy at sea, after the Second World War.

England engaged in a long struggle to consolidate her Empire and considered herself ruler of the seas in 1805, after having waged the decisive naval battle of Trafalgar on the 21st October 1805. Up to that date her supremacy was not complete, it was challenged, and she was even defeated in some wars, as in the case of the revolution of her large American Colony.

In 1588 the Invincible Armada of Felipe II of Spain was defeated. This is a very important historic fact which started to change the leadership at sea, a denial of the marxist theory of the primary importance of the economic aspects in human history. Without denying that this factor is extremely important, one can say that the genius of a great man, or his errors, or a group of human beings and their capacity, have been the cornerstones of basic historic events.

Don Alvaro de Bazán, Marquis of Santa Cruz, was the man who had created the powerful Invincible Armada, but his death left Spain without a leader, devoid of the man who had defeated the Turks in Lepanto and the British and French in the Mediterranean and the Atlantic, where he also evaluated the professional capability of the British leaders and thus achieved his great naval victory.

Queen Elizabeth's corsairs and pirates started to attack the enormous Spanish Empire and saw that it was vulnerable. France and Holland, the other two naval powers, set out to conquer the Spanish Americas as well as India and Asia, which were under Portuguese influence.

Even though already in the XVIth Century they started to capture Spanish positions, the British affirmed this tendency in the XVIIth Century. In that same period, the Spanish decline became more marked, attacked by England, France and Holland. At the end of the century, the Austrian dynasty, which had become weaker all the time, ended with the death of Carlos II, who was physically impaired and the last member of a powerful dynasty which had dominated the world. Spain was in danger, its fleet was non-existent, because it had become depleted fighting against the three maritime powers.

During this XVIIth Century England continued with its fruitful pirate expeditions and settled in the Antilles and in New England.

We can say that by then the Treaty of Tordesillas (signed on the 7th of June 1494) which protected the domains of Spain west of a line located 370 leagues from the Cape Verde Islands, was only a piece of paper insofar as the North Atlantic and the Caribbean were concerned; on the other hand, its validity in the South Atlantic and in the Pacific was to endure until the middle of the XVIIIth Century.

The War of Succession (1700—1713) was another great danger for the Spanish possessions, while the Bourbon Pretender, who was later to become Felipe V, was winning.

It was during this war that England occupied the strategically positioned Gibraltar, in the name of the Austrian Pretender. After this war was over, "The Rock" had to be returned to Spain, but England did not do so, and consolidated her position by means of the Treaty of Utrecht (1713), also obtaining Terranova, Acadia, the Hudson Bay and an exclusive right to the sale of negroes in America, which also allowed her to carry out profitable smuggling activities.

The Seven Years War ended with the Peace of Paris in 1763, which was very hard for France and allowed England to achieve the growth of her Empire through Canada. Let us also say that it was during this war that England attacked the River Plate for the first time, so as to achieve supremacy.

Already towards the end of the rule of Felipe V, the Spanish Armada had managed to get back something of its former power, which increased under Carlos III. This last monarch became the ally of France through the Family Pact of 1767 against England, but the hard struggle finished in 1805 with the absolute predominance of England, obtained through Nelson's genius in the battle of Trafalgar.

It is also true that England had definitely lost her colony in North America, the United States, but she still retained Canada.

The struggle for India passed from Portuguese predominance during almost all the XVIth Century to Holland, and then to England, who started to consolidate in the north in the middle of the XVIIIth Century.

In Australia, in New South Wales, England set up a penal settlement.

During the XIXth Century in the Victorian Period, the British Empire reached its greatest spendour.

After Trafalgar, a new world order appears, the British imperial order. Cape Town is taken in 1805; Buenos Aires repels the invader in 1806 and 1807 in one of the few defeats suffered by the English. Singapore becomes a powerful English base as of 1826; India is completely occupied by about 1850 and Queen Victoria is proclaimed Empress of India in 1877, Ceylon included. Australia, New Zealand, Canada and island possessions in the Antilles, Oceania and China complete the powerful Empire. In 1833 the Malvinas are also occupied by Britain. The empire building strategy had concluded and Britain held vast possessions to carry on trade with, bringing raw materials from the Colonies and returning manufactured products, all in English ships. Cromwell's Navigation Act of 1641 had made England the most important mercantile power. Her fleet was several times bigger than most of the world's merchant fleets together, permitting her to dominate world maritime commerce.

If we look at a map we can see that the only zone where all the oceans connect is situated in the Southern Hemisphere, in different latitudes which go from 0° to 60° S. It is exactly in the South of our territory where the passage is most southerly and narrowest. In Australia it passes both South and North, although, until now, the northern passage is more important. In South Africa it lies between 35° S. and the Antarctic. Britain, when forming its Empire, occupied all the peninsulas

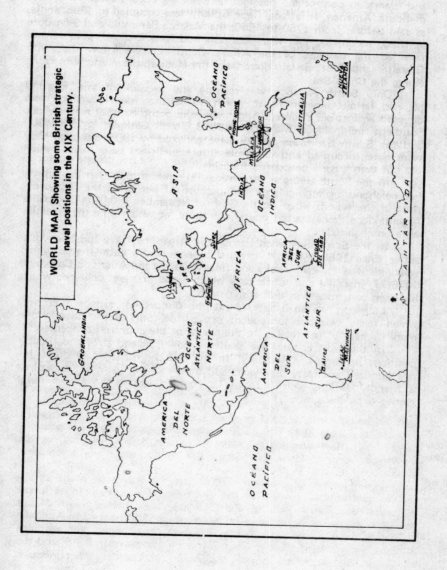

WORLD MAP. Showing some British strategic naval positions in the XIX Century.

and islands to control the passages between the oceans except one, that
of South America. In effect, Cape Colony was occupied in 1805; India,
as said before, from 1750 to 1850; the Malacca Peninsula and Singapore
in 1826, which, together with Australia and New Zealand, gave control
over all the passages of the Asiatic Continent. We know that with
Gibraltar and Suez, Britain dominated the Mediterranean and with Hong
Kong, the China Sea.

Only South America was missing and because of this, England
planned various expeditions of which no less than seven incursions were
directed against our country. And finally she occupied until recently our
Southern archipelagos. Malvinas in 1833, South Georgias in 1906/1908
and the South Sandwich Islands were annexed in 1908, although they
were never occupied and only scientific expeditions were made, which
did not even leave a beacon on the islands.

In the South Georgias, Argentina has rights through her proximity,
her neighbouring archipelagos and because of her being the first occu-
pant of the islands when on the 16th of November 1904 the Compañía
Argentina de Pesca started operations there, at which time the Georgias
were uninhabited.

In the South Sandwich Islands the Argentine Navy has been very
active since 1950, when it installed beacons and a naval shelter which
was inhabited for two weeks and finally, during the Antarctic Campaign
1976/77, installed a scientific base which is the first and only one which
has been constructed in that archipelago.

Later on we shall talk about the discoveries, supposed or not,
which really, without subsequent occupation, only served to add one
more element of sovereignty to the claims of the countries concerned.

In the next chapter we shall see how England strove to occupy
positions in Argentine territory. In the end she managed to do so for
one hundred and forty nine years and three months, in an action against
a friendly nation, which cannot be counted among the British naval
glories — on the contrary!

CHAPTER II

Argentina and Great Britain — Eight English Invasions

Argentina is the country which has lost more of its coastline than any other country in American history. Bolivia lost all of its Pacific coast, this is a fact, but Argentina lost a greater extension than that which Bolivia lost.

If we take as our basis that our original territory was that of the Viceroyalty of the Rio de la Plata, we have lost the maritime coast which goes from the Island of Santa Catarina up to the mouth of the Rio de la Plata and the banks of the Uruguay and Rio de la Plata Rivers, which now constitute the borders of Uruguay. In the South, as from 1810, we have lost at least half of the Magellan Straits.

Until 1826 the coast of Alto Peru (now Bolivia) on the Pacific belonged first, to the Viceroyalty, and later to the United Provinces of the Rio de la Plata. Also the port of Cobija belonged to the Jurisdiction of Salta.

Neither were we the owners of our great islands of the South Atlantic, like the Malvinas or the South Georgias, and our rights to the South Sandwich Islands have been challenged.

On the other hand, Brazil has her Trinidad Island one thousand kilometres away from Rio de Janeiro; Ecuador retains her Galapagos Islands 1,050 **kilometres** from her coast and Chile has Juan Fernandez Island and Easter Island, the latter more than 3,300 **kilometres** away from her continental coastline.

In general, almost all the American nations have retained their islands, althourgh Venezuela has lost Trinidad; but none has suffered or continues to suffer such a sustained and constant pressure from the British Empire as Argentina.

In the Spanish Colonial period, one can understand this pressure and attack against Spain. It was a case of struggle for predominance between Spain and France on one side; united through Bourbon family links and, as of 1761, through the Family Pact; and on the other, a thriving England, building up her Empire based on maritime power and industrial progress.

In the post-Colonial independent period, such aggression is far less justifiable. Argentina obtained her independence with English aid in arms and supplies. It is true that she had to pay the high price of economic dependence, but that was unavoidable, as we shall explain later.

We, the Argentines, were good friends of England. We became her supplier of hides, fats and meat; we adapted ourselves to her needs and requirements; but we were attacked in the Malvinas, in the South Atlantic and in the Antarctic in times of peace.

Times changed, Argentina achieved her economic independence, but the irritating British presence continued in parts of our territory.

Not everything was negative while England dominated our economy, nor can we but admire the greatness of her human endeavour and the vigour of her democratic institutions, as well as her defence of freedom in the last two World Wars; but the nation of Nelson, Wellington and Churchill, that of Locke and Shakespeare, should recognize that another nation which has produced San Martin, Belgrano, Brown, Rivadavia, Mitre, Sarmiento and Roca, could not abide the continued occupation of the Malvinas, and the Southern and Antarctic Islands based on arguments sustained by force.

This loss of coastline and islands by Argentina through pressure, the biggest ever exerted by the "ruler of the waves" against any South American country, undoubtedly has other causes as well, but the British actions have been a decisive factor.

Our lack of maritime awareness, stemming from colonial problems and the existence of vast and rich tracts of land, sparsely populated, turned our thoughts landward, but we reacted in time, and adapted to the sea.

What were the reasons that made England intervene more in Argentina than in other South American countries? We believe there are various reasons and shall expain them briefly. Undoubtedly there was the basic political motive of consolidating the power of the British Empire in a rich and important area of great potential.

We also consider that geopolitical and naval motives were important, as the South Atlantic was an ocean of increasing strategic importance and England was interested in controlling parts of Argentina, like Patagonia, the Malvinas or the Antarctic Peninsula, like she controlled Singapore, India, Ceylon, South Africa and Gibraltar, as through the former she would have control over the passage between the South Atlantic and the South Pacific. This route started to acquire enormous importance as from the end of the XVIth Century until 1914, when the Panama Canal was opened. Its potential importance continued to exist, however, and now it increases again in the light of the possibility of the closure of the Panama Canal due to sabotage, or due to the availability of supertankers, bulk grain or ore carriers, whose breadth would prevent them from using the Panama Canal.

The growing economic importance of Argentina and its seas became reasons for further aggresions. Ever since 1680, when Don Manuel Lobo founded Colonia del Sacramento, which was an advance base for Portuguese penetration into the Rio de la Plata, it became the biggest center for contraband in the Viceroyalty. Buenos Aires then expanded thanks to the smuggling activities carried out by the English, the Portuguese, the Dutch and the French. The Authorities turned a blind eye and the losers were the merchants and Spanish trade. That was the time also, when the potential capacity of Buenos Aires and its hinterland was discovered, mainly for cattle raising. Furthermore, the silver from Potosi began to arrive at, and leave, from Buenos Aires. Abundant livestock, plenty of hides, horns, lard, salt beef were all obtainable and were sold cheaply, as well as all kinds of manufactured products which were unavailable in the Viceroyalty, especially quality textiles.

England was the first nation to have the industrial revolution and as from 1770, for thirty to fifty years, she was ahead of the rest of Europe. Having excess production, she had to seek markets to place her products, and if these were colonies, all the better. And if, furthermore, she could obtain cheap raw materials in return from these markets, better still. The Rio de la Plata offered everything and had an extraordinary potential.

Then another economic circumstance came to the forefron insofar as the "English maritime invasion" was concerned: namely, the abundance of whales and seals in our Patagonian and Malvinian waters.

From the third decade of the XVIIIth Century until the present day, firstly the British, then the Americans, French, Norwegians, Dutch and South Africans have been devastating our seas of hundreds of thousands of cetaceans and of several million seals, and have gone so far as to make some species almost extinct.

Today the same thing is still happening, but compounded by the Russians and the Japanese.

Let us then quickly review these English invasions, highlighting only some of the less well-known aspects or expressing opinions which might be new.

The First English Invasion (1763)

The mention of only one date defines the peak efforts of a prolonged intention, for we can say that for almost a century, from 1680 to 1777, England assisted, encouraged or was engaged in a continuous attack on the Viceroyalty of the Rio de la Plata, either as declared ally of the Portuguese aggressor, or through powerful diplomatic action in times of peace, or through direct action, all in the North-East and in the Rio de la Plata areas.

As from its founding in 1680, the port of Colonia del Sacramento became the centre of Portuguese and also English contraband.

In 1703, through the Methuen Treaty, England and Portugal formed a commercial and political alliance which was to produce important successes for both powers. This close alliance, faithfully observed until 1911, is one of the longest and most noteworthy in modern history. Portugal continued in interdependence with the triumphant English and obtained, in return, many benefits which she would not have attained on her own.

Regarding the Viceroyalty, we may say that the Anglo-Portuguese action was exercised in combination with the Portuguese in the North-East; in the Rio de la Plata zone, with the Portuguese as principal protagonists, and by the English alone in Patagonia and the South Atlantic Islands, where they occupied Port Egmont in the Malvinas.

As soon as the founding, by the Portuguese, of Colonia del Sacramento became known in Buenos Aires, the then Governor ordered an expedition to be sent to expel them, and after bloody combat, the town was taken on the 7th of August 1680. The brilliant and complete victory was cancelled out by diplomatic actions, and in February 1683, Colonia del Sacramento was restored to the Portuguese.

During the war of the Spanish Succession, the town was taken again on the 14th of May 1705, fundamentally through the actions of the men of Buenos Aires. After the Peace of Utrecht, and through England's influence, it was returned again to the Portuguese. in 1716. The Methuen Treaty was working.

In 1735 Colonia was besieged until 1737, when a Peace Convention put an end to this siege.

The Treaty of Utrecht of 1713 gave the English the slave traffic in America and the opportunity to intrude economically in Buenos Aires until 1739.

Fernando VI, married to Doña Barbara de Braganza, was influenced by his wife and favoured Portugal in his policy, to the detriment of Spanish interests. The Treaty of the 13th of January 1750, called the "Barter" or "Madrid" Treaty, obtained the promise to return Colonia in exchange for large advances by the Portuguese in Rio Grande and Paraguay. It included the deplorable clause of the handing over of the seven Jesuit Missions, unjust by all lights, and which precipitated the War of the Missions. Because of this war, a powerful naval expedition came to the Rio de la Plata, under Don Pedro de Cevallos, the last great Spanish champion in the Americas towards the end of the XVIIIth Century.

The War of the Jesuit Missions was the pretext for Portugal not to return Colonia del Sacramento, but moreover she had managed to break and remove the Tordesillas line legally, given that she had been infringing it for more than a century.

The "Barter" Treaty was suspended in 1761 and Cevallos commenced hostilities against Colonia, which he besieged and overcame on the 2nd of November 1762, employing his military prowess and great qualities as a warrior and leader. Soon he had to defend himself from an

Anglo-Portuguese attack, which, after a century of aggression, we will call the First English Invasion, even if it really was Anglo-Portuguese.

The Portuguese ambassador in London organized a veritable expedition of conquest to the Rio de la Plata. Its purpose was to occupy military positions and convert the zone of Colonia into an Anglo-Portuguese centre of commerce, a sort of enclave in the Rio de la Plata area. To this purpose, and with the participation of the English East India Company, a subscription was floated which raised 100,000 pounds sterling, loading ships with cloth and merchandise so as to combine commercial advantages with the military campaign.

John MacNamara, a brave and experienced adventurer, was the leader of the expedition and he armed a ship, the "Lord Clive" for his own account, with 64 guns and sold it to the Admiralty. Also the 40 gun frigate "Ambuscade" (Captain Roberts) was readied and 700 men were embarked between troops and seamen.

The ships sailed from England in July 1762 and went to Lisbon, where ranks and honours were assigned, and finally they sailed for Rio de Janeiro on the 30th of August 1762. At this stage the Count of Bobadilla, the Governor, added the powerful reinforcements of a man-of-war, the "Gloria" with 60 guns, as well as one frigate and six brigs, and 600 troopers. The expedition was really an invasion aimed to stay. It was the most powerful naval force ever to have been prepared against the Rio de la Plata.

The invaders arrived at Maldonado at the beginning of December 1762 and there seized a small Spanish boat which informed them of the surrender of Colonia.

On the 4th of December they were off Montevideo and tried to sail up to Buenos Aires, but the Rio de la Plata, with its currents and shallows, impeded this. The 2nd of January they took up stations off Montevideo with the intention of attacking the city, but the following day a pilot arrived from Rio de Janeiro and informed them that the ships were of too deep a draft to enter Montevideo and so they decided to attack Colonia.

Meanwhile Cevallos, very sick with malaria, was in Colonia and split his troops between Maldonado and Montevideo, leaving 500 men in Colonia and 100 in the isle of San Gabriel.

On the 6th of January 1763 Commodore MacNamara led the attack on the Fort of Santa Rita with the "Lord Clive", the "Ambuscade" attacked Fort San Pedro and the "Gloria" Fort San Miguel.

The bombardment started at midday and was intense, but the Cevallos troops, sheltered behind low parapets, did not suffer many casualties because the enemy shots were very high.

The firing was very heavy, the attacking ships used more than 3,000 cannon balls, crossbar shot and grapeshot and from land, they replied with equal intensity.

At 4 p.m. the "Lord Clive", which already had lost 40 out of her 500 men, was set on fire by a shot from land, without doubt, by a red-hot cannon ball, heated up before firing. The fire spread and could not be contained, burning the ship completely and most of her crew perished, either burnt to death or drowned. Eighty men were saved by swimming and two escaped in a small boat; as for MacNamara, he died in the fire or, according to another version, was wounded and flung himself into the water, where he drowned.

The other ships, which had been severely punished, especially the frigate "Ambuscade", withdrew. The "Gloria" and the other smaller Portuguese ships were also slightly damaged, although they had not ventured so much into combat. The frigate suffered 80 dead and many wounded and the Portuguese naval division retired toward Rio de Janeiro. A small Spanish naval detachment also took part in the action, but its performance was poor.

The Peace of Paris of 1763, whereat the decisive English influence favoured Portugal, decided on another delivery of the area to Portugal.

With the Portuguese attacks from 1773 onwards, and especially that of 1775 on Rio Grande, the struggle was renewed, and furthermore, the occupation by the English of Port Egmont, in the South, made Spain create the Viceroyalty of the Rio de la Plata.

Don Pedro de Cevallos was appointed first Viceroy, and sailed with 20 warships, among them six new and powerful men-of-war, 96 merchant ships and more than 9,500 troops, which, with the crew, totalled 20,000 men. In addition, there were 600 guns and plenty of supplies. This mighty fleet, the most powerful ever to be seen in our waters, took Santa Catalina and besieged and took Colonia in 1777.

This powerful expedition, coupled with the military genius of Cevallos, finished off the war for more than thirty years and it only flared up again after independence.

The Second English Invasion (1765—1774)

This was almost simultaneous with the first one, but was carried out exclusively by England in our South Atlantic.

The Southern parts of our territory began to be coveted by the French and the British as from the beginning of the XVIIIth Century.

Toward the end of the XVIIth Century, corsairs and pirates started to visit the Malvinas. It should also be noted that Dutch marauders were found about the islands as from the end of the XVIth Century, but mainly when they were en route to the Pacific.

The English visited our waters as from 1683 with the adventurers William Dampier, John Cook and Ambrose Cowley, all in the same ship. In 1690 John Strong visited the Malvinas and named the strait which separated the two main islands Falkland Sound.

Then in 1708 the islands were sighted by the English corsair Woodes Rogers.

In 1711 en article was written which was published more than twenty years later in London with the allusive title: "A proposal for humbling Spain — written in 1711 by a person of distinction". It proposed sending an expedition of 2,500 men to take Buenos Aires and it gave details of the riches and produce of the country. Admiral Anson's expedition in 1739/40 pointed out the need to occupy the Malvinas and other points in our Patagonia.

There were greater possibilities for British action in the islands however and added to the geopolitical and strategic interests, there was a commercial incentive: the hunting of whales and seals which swarmed around the islands.

The English seal and whale hunters started an intensive depredation as from the middle of the XVIIth Century: They started in the Malvinas and continued on the Patagonian coasts, as far as Cape Horn, Isla de los Estados, etc.

With the presence of Commodore John Byron in the Malvinas in 1765, an English penetration was initiated in 1766 which lasted until 1774. Later on we shall deal with this.

The Third and Fourth English Invasions (1806—1807)

These are the invasions usually known as the First and Second Invasions in our schools. They are sufficiently well known and we shall only refer to their consequences.

Carlos Roberts, in his book "The English Invasions of the Rio de la Plata (1806—1807)" describes various planned English invasions. In several of them Don Francisco Miranda, illustrious forerunner of the independence of the Americas, was involved. There were plans, orders and even traces of invasions which did not prosper in 1789/1790, in 1799/1801, and in 1803.

After the Battle of Trafalgar on the 21st of October 1805, England acquired complete control of the seas, greatly superior to that of her rivals, France and Spain. England dominated the seas and Napoleonic France dominated the Continent. As from 1804, Spain had entered the fray on the side of her old ally, France.

At Trafalgar, between them, France and Spain lost 19 ships, which was not in itself a decisive fact, but was when added to a long series of defeats and the loss of morale in the face of the superior material, crews and tactics displayed by the English. Spain had lost far more ships in her home bases, where they lay rotting because there were no funds for repairs.

After Trafalgar, the English had more than 130 ships in service, whereas Spain and France had less than 90 between them in total, and only 60 of them were fit for active service. The English superiority was absolute and she retained mastery of the seas for more than a century. This superiority permitted Commodore Sir Home Popham "tam Marte quam Mercurio", an unusual character who believed the time was ripe at the end of 1805, to make a foray against Buenos Aires. Sailing from Cape Town, he decided to make a try, according to the latest English plan that he was aware of, being sure of the support he would get if he succeeded.

Both English invasions of 1806 and 1807 were due to the English policy of that time, which matched the permanent imperialistic policy: to acquire an important colony of great strategic value and a market with a big future and which, moreover, could absorb the industrial surpluses. Both invasions were important amphibious operations, especially the second, which is comparable only to that of Don Pedro de Cevallos in 1776/1777.

These two amphibious operations were able to be developed with absolute serenity in the naval phase, thanks to the recently acquired mastery of the seas.

The naval force which attacked Buenos Aires was powerful: two ships with 64 guns, two frigates, 1 brig and five armed transports – these were too much for the Spanish naval forces of the Rio de la Plata, composed of old or weak units and gunboats. In fact, the Spaniards only had one light corvette, 1 brig, three schooners, two sloops and 25 launches mounted with guns. The disproportion was so great that just one English ship of 64 guns surpassed the fire-power of all the Spanish force. For this reason, the Spanish sailors fought on land, which they did bravely and tenaciously.

The English land force consisting of 1,641 men, on the other hand, was too small to overcome a city of nearly 50,000 souls, counting the inhabitants of the environs. Therein lay the English weakness and Captain Santiago de Liniers, the guiding spirit of the Reconquista, was the man who perceived it.

Starting with 1,000 men from the Banda Oriental (now Uruguay), the recapture was achieved between the 5th and the 12th of August 1806 and the hero was Liniers, who had become both the military and the civil authority, in the absence of the Viceroy.

While their troops were surrendering in the Fort, the English fleet could not help them because sandbanks close to the city kept the fleet away and the guns did not have enough range to cooperate with the troops. The Rio de la Plata had helped to impede the English attack with one of its South-Eastern winds and its sandbanks which prevented the English ships from attacking the opposing ships.

When the bountiful booty captured in Buenos Aires arrived in London a trumphant welcome was given and the popularity of Sir Home

Popham equalled that of some of England's greatest heroes. The news of the defeat was terrible and the reaction to it was to renew the conflict. A basic fact emerged from the Rio de la Plata operation: in all the time between the Spanish recapture of Buenos Aires and the second English attack, the British fleet was in control of the river without any dispute. This historical proof of the great importance of naval power should always be borne in mind by us.

The English invasion of 1807 was made with superior forces, gathered in various expeditions.

The fleet commanded by Vice-Admiral George Murray was composed of five men-of-war of 64 guns each, five frigates with a total of 150 guns, 12 minor ships which totalled 175 guns. All this made up a naval force of 23 or 34 warships with over 650 guns. The transports, many of them armoured, were more than 50. The troops totalled about 15,000 men, some of them in the Banda Oriental.

After taking Maldonado and then Montevideo, the English landed at Ensenada on the 27th of June 1807 with over 9,000 men and 16 pieces of artillery. They were under the command of Lieutenant General John Whitelocke.

We already know that on the Spanish side, Liniers was in command of an army of 8,000 men, ready for the defence with 49 guns of various calibers.

The final English attack was carried out at dawn on a cold 5th of July 1807, after Liniers had committed a bad tactical mistake by crossing the Riachuelo and the being defeated at Miserere.

Between 5,021 and 5,787 English were readied and attacked the 8,000 Spaniards and locals (criollos). The invading forces were warhardened veterans, the Spanish were green and some were only armed with swords.

After capturing the Plaza de Toros with superior forces against a heroic resistance, the rest of the troops were defeated by the criollos, with the help of all the civilian inhabitants, who fought against the invading forces, causing heavy casualties as they passed through the city.

El Retiro and Plaza de Toros were the scenes of the most bloody resistance, since the total casualties of the defenders (dead, wounded and missing) reached 27 % and those of the English were 20 %. In the

In the rest of the line the defenders lost almost 8 % and the English 23 %.

The English effort in the invasion was huge and the preparation of another, more powerful one, was begun, but not concluded as Spain became allied to Britain when her territories were occupied by Napoleon's forces.

The commercial expectations are shown by the ships, loaded to the top with English goods, especially textiles, which entered Montevideo during the few months of occupation.

Year 1807 – Ships that entered Montevideo port.

February	:	78
March	:	27
April	:	18
May	:	5
June	:	4
Total	:	132

It was a parallel commercial invasion. A great part of the merchandise was badly sold, after the new defeat. Buenos Aires knew its most glorious hour and clearly learnt of the courage of its sons. The two great victories were a foretaste of the May Revolution. We shall deal with the rest in detail further on.

The Fifth English Invasion (3rd of January 1833)

We shall deal with this further on.

The Sixth English Invasion (1845–1847)

This English invasion is part of the Anglo-French blockades, from 1838 to 1840 by the French and from 1845 to 1847, with English cooperation. France continued alone until 1848.

We, the Argentines, continued to be engaged in civil war and Rosas was dictator. His handling of French subjects and later English, whom he wanted to incorporate into his armies, provided the pretext for French, and later English, intervention. Both powers were waiting for the opportunity to occupy some zones or to install profitable commercial companies in the country.

The blockades lasted for 2,000 days and Buenos Aires remained closed to commerce during this time. We could do nothing against such a powerful force of modern ships, frigates, corvettes and brigs with new and efficient artillery. Nevertheless, national honour was upheld.

The most important events were the capture on the 2nd of August 1845 of the small Argentine naval force under the command of Admiral Brown; sallies up the rivers, especially by Garibaldi, and the Battle of Obligado, always honourable in Argentine history.

The Battle of Obligado was fought on the river Paraná on the 20th of November 1845. The Anglo-French force consisted of three powerful ships and eight small sailing boats with a hundred pieces of modern artillery, some of which fired Paixhans grenades with fuses.

The action was bloody and the criollo troops who were defending their native land behaved with heroism even though they had only old guns of small calibre.

The chain which obstructed the river was defended by a few boats and launches which were soon attacked and eliminated. The action started at 09.00 and the four federal batteries, three of them commanded by navy officers Alvaro de Alzogaray, Juan B. Thorne and Eduardo Brown, son of the Admiral; and the fourth by an Army officer, Felipe Palacio, fought until the ammunition ran out, under very heavey fire which caused them great casualties. The chain was finally cut and at 17.00 Thorne's, the last battery still in action, ran out of ammunition.

At almost 18.00 the allied troops landed and General Mansilla made a bayonet charge on them, but fell wounded. Other Criollo charges, including a cavalry charge, had some success, but in the end were finally repulsed.

The Allies had suffered a hundred casualties and had several ships damaged, the Argentine losses were 240 men.

Rosas was the Argentine governor to whom the Argentine Provinces had delegated their foreign relations, but in Obligado the battle was fought by a united Argentina.

A large convoy made up of a large ship escorted by three warships made a difficult voyage up the Paraná, but the battles of Tonelero, San Lorenzo and Quebracho showed the Allies that Argentina would not yield.

The Peace signed was honourable for our country but did not compensate the sacrifices and losses.

1908 until the present day

This seventh English invasion comes about as a result of the whaling industry centered in the Georgias, which we will deal with further on.

The Eighth English Invasion — 2nd April 1982 (and still continues)

This began with the despatch of a powerful English fleet which took the Georgias on the 25th of April but encountered a resistance which still continues.

On the 30th of April a combined air and sea attack was made on the Malvinas and at the time of writing the action still continues.

Conclusions

For almost four centuries these regions, Spanish or Argentine, have been subject to permanent British aggression.

1) From 1680 to 1777, with an attack in 1765 in the Rio de la Plata and the North East.

2) From 1750 until the present day, with occupations in 1765 to 1774, and from 1833 until now, in Patagonia and the Malvinas.

3) By direct attacks with two large amphibious expeditions, in 1806 and 1807 with a blockade in the Rio de la Plata and tributaries area.

4) By acquiring an enormous Antactic-Subantarctic sector from 1908 until the present time.

Argentina, in 1810, fell under British commercial and economic control, because not only was the Royal Navy absolute ruler of the seas, but the merchant navy was several times larger than all the rest of the world's put together. With the elimination of the Spanish merchant navy, Argentina unavoidably fell under English maritime domination.

We have now attained our economic independence as much as is possible in this interdependent world of ours today, but for more than a century we suffered the English influence.

For geopolitical, strategic, naval and economic reasons, England has coveted our territory. She attacked the continental part without success, but she seized our islands and dominated part of our seas. It is a consequence of her maritime power and her right is based on the use of force.

CHAPTER III

Brief geographical description of the Malvinas

The Malvinas are an archipelago of almost 12,000 square kilometers, 300 miles from the Argentine mainland, somewhat to the North of the entrance to the Straits of Magellan. The group is formed by two main islands and many smaller ones.

Rio Gallegos, capital of Santa Cruz, is on the same latitude, that is on the same parallel as the capital of the islands, and approximately 760 kilometers away, but only 555 kms from the nearest island of the archipelago.

Cape San Juan de Salvamento in the Isla de los Estados is the closest point between our coast and Cape Belgrano in the southwest of the Gran Malvina island. The distance between them is 346 kilometers.

The two principal islands are Soledad, the largest, to the East, and Gran Malvina. They are separated by the San Carlos Channel. There are 15 islands of more than 20 kms. each, about a hundred including the smaller ones and almost two hundred, if one includes the islets.

In latitude, that is from East to West, the Malvinas cover a distance similar to that existing between the seaside resorts of Monte Hermoso and Miramar. In longitude, that is from North to South, they cover an area like the one between the Coig Estuary and Dungeness Point in the territory of Santa Cruz. Thus, from East to West they cover 259 kilometers and 159 kilometers from North to South. If we picture a rectangle of this size, about a quarter of it will be occupied by land and the rest by water. The coastline of the islands is very indented with deep estuaries and depressions in all directions.

The Malvinas are on Argentina's continental shelf, that means the are joined to Patagonia by a submarine platform not more than 200 meters deep, and as they are part of our continental shelf they are part of our territory.

Geology

The geology of the Malvinas is very similar to that of Patagonia, but it has some unique features as the absence of very old soil. Most of the soil was formed during the middle and end of the Paleozoic, the Mezozoic and Cenozoic eras.

Covering the hard, precambrian basis, which is only visible in Cape

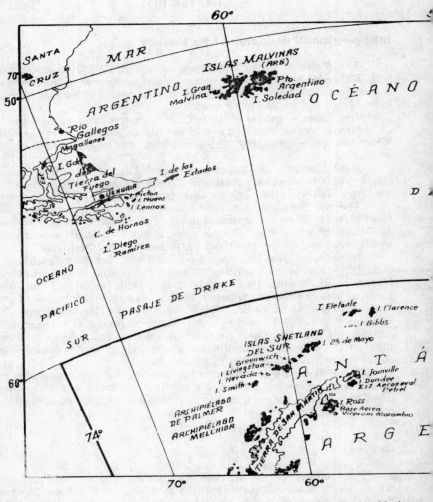

Our southern archipelagos.

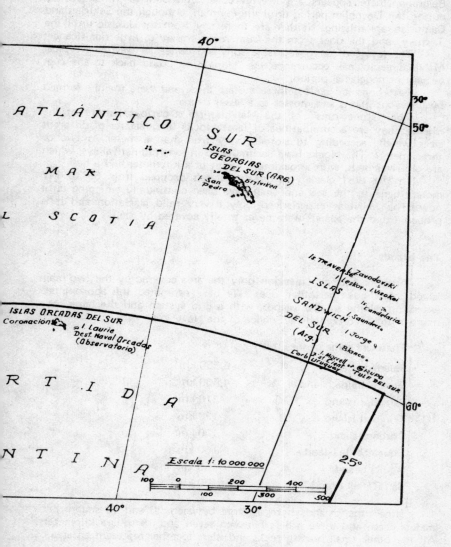

ATLÁNTICO

SUR

MAR

L SCOTIA

ISLAS
GEORGIAS
DEL SUR (ARG)
I. Brylviken
I. San
Pedro

Is TRAVERSÉ I. Zavodoski
I. Leskor. I. Visokoi
ISLAS
Is. Candelaria
SANDWICH I. Saunders
DEL SUR I. Jorge
(Arg.) I. Blanco.
I. Morrell ó GRUPO
Corb.(Uruguay) TULE DEL SUR

ISLAS ORCADAS DEL SUR
Coronación. I. Laurie
Dest. Naval Orcadas
(Observatorio)

RT I D A

NTIN A

Escala 1: 10 000 000

100   0   200   400
     100   300   500

40°

30°

50°

60°

25°

40°   30°

Belgrano, there appears a powerful cover of sediments which started during the Devonian period until the Permian, although the Selurian and Cambrian are missing. Neither are there any from the Jurasic until the Tertiary, and the ones from the Cuaternary era are of little significance.

The layers of peat, vegetable soils and dunes, as well as a typical Malvinas geological occurrence, the "stone runs" date back to the cuaternary or neoglacial period.

Peat bogs are almost three meters thick and were mainly formed by liliaceous plants and mosses to a lesser degree.

The "stone runs" of the Malvinas are a curious feature of the islands, they are accumulations of large blocks of quartzite of different sizes which, according to Borello, vary from half a meter to two or three meters. The blocks have accumulated in longitudinal valleys, which are old river beds, with a maximum width of a kilometer and a half.

In the post glacial period the islands dropped from 69 to 117 meters beneath the sea and then have been continually emerging until now. The Malvinas experienced only a very mild glaciation and it is probable that the islands were never totally covered by ice.

The Islands

Authors normally mention only the area covered by the two main islands, but not the other ones. We have estimated the approximate extension of the smaller islands, with a grid system and the large scale maps of the Hydrographical Service of the Navy.

These are some of the sizes:

Soledad Island	6,350 km^2
Gran Malvina Island	4,500 km^2
San Jose Island	270 km^2
Trinidad Island	120 km^2
Borbon Island	100 km^2
Bougainville Island	60 km^2
Aguila Island	55 km^2
San Rafael Island	50 km^2

Nine other islands have an area between 20 and 45 square kilometers each, and three others between seven and 18 square kilometers. All the other small islands, rocks and islets together represent an area of 80 square kilometers.

The archipelago is quite large, its size is equivalent to half of the

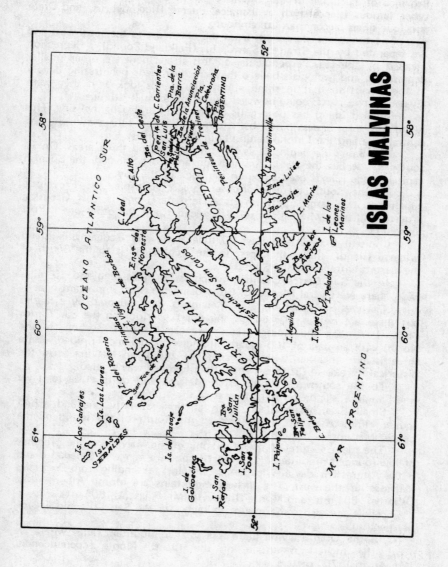

ISLAS MALVINAS

Province of Tucuman or the Territory of Isla del Fuego and larger than other famous islands such as Jamaica, Puerto Rico, Cyprus, and Crete and four times bigger than Luxembourg.

The two main islands run from the northeast to the southwest and are separated by the Strait of San Carlos (Falkland Sound), a depression invaded by the sea. Perpendicular to this strait there are other smaller depressions and geologists believe they are river beds penetrating deeply in the islands so that in some places the islands look as if they were divided in two parts, being however joined by a small isthmus.

Soledad island has deep gulfs on the San Carlos Channel side. This island has three areas joined by isthmus: the San Luis peninsula, the central area and the Lafone peninsula in the southeast.

The San Luis peninsula is the smallest of the three areas. On its southern side lies the Bahia Anunciacion and Port Soledad, the Spanish capital of the islands used to be on the back of the bay.

To the South there is another larger peninsula, the Freycinet, which has two large inlets on its eastern part, one is Port Groussac (Puerto Williams) where the capital is located and the other one is Port Enriqueta.

Choiseul Sound is almost 20 miles long and Bougainville island (Liberty island), the sixth largest in the archipelago is to the South of the eastern entrance to the Sound.

In the San Carlos Channel, which is 50 miles long and 10 miles wide, there are several islands, El Cisne being the most important one.

The western coast of Gran Malvina is very indented by estuaries but these are not as marked on the coast overlooking the San Carlos Channel. Among the closest islands we can mention, Borbon, to the North, with an area of 100 square kilometers; Vigia and Trinidad. These three islands together with the coast of the Gran Malvina form the historical Port de la Cruzada (where Port Egmont was located).

To the southwest of the Gran Malvina and quite close to it we find San Jose island, the third largest of the archipelago.

Small Beauchesne island, with an area of only one and a half square kilometer is 26 kilometers to the South of the island of the Leones Marinos.

The main feature of the orography of the Malvinas is the presence of low-rounded mountains. The most important range in Soledad island is the Alturas Rivadavia (Wickham mountains), extending from Port Islas Malvinas to the west. The highest mountains are Monte Alberdi (Mt. Osborne), 684 mts. and Monte Rivadavia (Mt. Pleasant), 605 mts.

There are also some mountain ranges in the San Luis and Freycinet peninsulas.

In the Gran Malvina there is a smaller mountain range where we find the highest mountain of the island, Monte Independencia, (Mt. Adams), 700 meters.

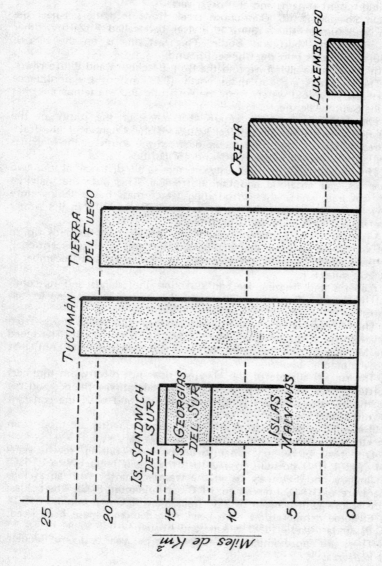

Comparison of three Argentine archipelagos of the South Atlantic with other geographic zones.

In the Malvinas there are no real rivers, but there are many creeks, short intermitent streams and also dry rivers.

On Soledad island, Caprichoso creek flows into the sea near the capital, and further south there is a river bed called Fitz Roy, other rivers are Pedro, Melo and Bodie. This last one is on the Lafone peninsula and flows into the Choiseul Sound.

In the Gran Malvina we find the Bull, Brackburn and Piloto rivers.

The Malvinas are 450 miles north (833 kms) of the confluence between the very cold waters from the Antarctic and the temperate ones from the South Atlantic.

The Malvinas are also about 450 miles to the south of the confluence between the subtropical waters of the Atlantic of the Brazilian stream and the colder ones coming from the south of the Malvinas stream, approximately between 40° and 45° latitude.

The archipelago is practically at the same distance of the two confluences, the antarctic and the subtropical. This puts the Malvinas within an area where the surrounding water mass has a temperature ranging in the south and the north between 3° and 10°C in the winter and between 4° and 6° to 14°C in summer.

In August and September the Antarctic ice pack extends up to 150 miles South east of the archipelago, but this is only exceptional, since the average limit of the ice pack in November and December is about 250 miles S.E.

Icebergs and floating ice can surround the islands and its continental shelf and when this happens the big chunks of floating ice are grounded.

The Malvinas stream is an enormous liquid mass which moves from the islands taking the cold subantarctic waters to the north. The speed of the Malvinas stream fluctuates, but it is approximately one knot, that is to say a mile an hour.

The rugged climate of the Malvinas does not offer warm summers nor bitterly cold winters; the ocean has a moderating influence and the winds modify the weather. It is damp. cloudy and with the constant harrassment of the wind.

Prevailing winds are from the west, less frequently are those from the north and southeast, and easterly winds are very rare.

On the basis of observations made during seven years (1944—1950) it is possible to say that the mean temperature is 6°C, with January and February being the warmer months with an average temperature of 10°C, (maximum 13°C and minimum 6°C). The coldest month is July with a mean of 2°C (maximum 4°C and minimun 1°C).

Extreme temperatures have been recorded and these have been: 24°C in January and −11°C in June and August.

There are approximately 54 foggy days per year and very frequently it is overcast.

Average rainfall during the above mentioned period (1944–1950) was 668,1 mm. and it rains uniformly all year round. It rains often but it does not pour. In winter it frequently snows, about 10 days per month, but very rarely between December and March. The climate is rugged, subantarctic, oceanic, which actually means cold, without much variation in temperature, windy and humid.

Flora and Fauna

The fact that the Malvinas are islands located in the subantarctic area and separated from the continent explain why they have a flora and fauna with some characteristics that differentiate it from that of Patagonia and Tierra del Fuego.

The marine flora of the Malvinas is based on fitoplankton, which is formed with diatoms or unicelullar algae with chlorophyll, foraminifers, and other very small organisms.

The diatoms are the basis of marine food, the "grass of the sea".

There are other more evolved algae, some of them are huge, being the largest one of all the Macrosystis pyrifera, the longest plant in the world.

Regarding land vegetation, the first impression one receives is that it is treeless except for the ones which have been planted by man in protected areas.

But the islands have many flowering plants, and they also have excellent grass.

The fauna is much richer and of greater variation and sea life is numerous and interesting.

The small crustaceans of the Euphasia Group which make up the "krill" are very abundant south of the Antarctic confluence and become more scarce as one goes north.

On the waters surrounding the Malvinas there are many invertebrates, like jellyfish, crustaceans like the "centolla" or southern king crab, sea urchins and mollusks. There are almost a hundred species of marine mollusks and 45 of them are endemic to the Malvinas.

Small octopus, squids, mollusks and small fish are the food of finned mamals, birds and some types of whales.

Among the fish we will mention tailed hakes, brotola, pollack, southern cod and pampanos, also different kinds of rays.

Seabirds belong to two classes, the ones which fly and the ones which do not and they are represented by many species.

Among the flying seabirds we can mention albatross, gulls, cormorants, etc., and among the flightless ones, the penguins.

Cormorants have long necks and underdeveloped wings, they frequent coastal waters and when flying skim within inches of the water.

The Malvinas species include the rock cormorant, the black shag and the king cormorant. The royal cormorant has a black back, white breast and a crest.

Robert Cushman Murphy refers to three types of geese and two of steamer ducks, as frequent visitors to the islands.

The predator of the islands is the brown skua of the Malvinas.

Gulls, terns and swallows are very numerous along the coasts of the islands. The snowy sheathbill (chionis alba) is small and has white feathers, has a short and slow flight and can also be seen in the islands.

Four types of penguins have been observed in the Malvinas, the king penguin, gentoo penguin, rockhopper and Magellanic penguin. The king penguin (aptenodytes patagonicus) is the second in size and is smaller than the emperor penguin.

The gentoo penguin (pygoscelis papua) is easily spotted because of its reddish-orange bill and prominent white spot on his black head.

The rockhoppers are smaller than the papuas, they are about 60 cm. tall. Their head is black with two yelow crests on the top.

The Magellanic penguin (sphneiscus magellanicus), also called "Jackass" in the Malvinas is 70 cm. tall. The back is dark grey, head and throat black with a "U" shaped band on the head and another white one on the shoulder.

The Malvinas finned mammals (seals and sea lions) belong to two families, the otaridae and phocidae.

The otaridae receive this name because they have small external ears, are more similar to carnivorous mammals and walk better on land. They are the southern sea lion and the southern fur seal.

The phocidae are fusiform and better adapted to swim, live and glide in the water. On land they drag themselves with problems. They are represented by the seals and elephant seals. In the Malvinas they are represented by elephant seals and leopard seals.

The southern fur seal (artocephalus australis) has been hunted for its very fine fur to make coats.

Southern sea lions can be almost four meters long and the males have a dark-brown mane.

Elephant seals (mirounga leonina) are the biggest among the finned mammals and belong to the phocidae, even though in some zoos they are classified as belonging to a different subfamily, that of the oystohorinae.

Leopard seals (hidruga leptonyx) are the fiercest and more carnivorous among the finned mammals and mainly feed on penguins, killing them in large numbers.

Many years ago there were many whales around the Malvinas where they found their favorite food, krill. Toothed whales like the sperm whale found abundant octopus and squids to eat there.

The blue whale is the largest animal alive. It can be 30 meters long and weigh up to 150 tons, equivalent to 25 elephants or 150 bulls (J. Marchowski, quoted by R. Lebedev). It feeds mainly on krill and can yield up to 84 to 89 barrels of oil. It has whalebones or baleens.

Until the end of the last century there were hundreds of thousands of them in the southern and antarctic seas. Today there are only several hundreds and they'll probably be extinct.

The finner whale or common rorqual is slightly smaller than the blue whale, it can be 25 meters long and weigh 80 tons.

The sei whale or Rudolphi's rorqual is similar to the common rorqual, but smaller because it is only 18 meters long.

The humpback whale, has a long fin, a big head and two breastbones, one in the centre and the other in the back giving it an appearance which justifies its name. It can be up to 37 meters long and weigh 30 tons.

The piked whale or lesser rorqual, is about 10 meters long.

Toothed whales are represented by the sperm whale, killer whale and dolphins. The sperm whale has a very large head, about a third of its total size, and can be about 20 meters long and has 25 pairs of teeth.

The killer whale is between 7 and 9 meters long and the females are smaller, about 5 meters long.

In the Malvinas the land fauna is not as rich as marine fauna.

Insects living in the islands belong to almost 70 genus or 90 species, of which about 60 % are endemic. The most numerous ones are the choleopterous, then the butterflies and the dipterous.

Spiders belong to six different species and are all endemic to the islands.

Land birds belong to approximately 75 genus of which 13 are permanent residents of the islands.

There is an upland goose with very tasty meat and also the kelp goose. Other birds are the least grebe, the Malvinas coot, the two-banded plover, the peregrine falcon, the black-neck swan, the crested duck, the Chilean wigeon and the silver teal.

There are also common snipes, black crown night herons, blackish cinclodes, ruffous-chested dotterel, Magellanic plover, etc. The predators are represented by a Malvinas chimango caracara and a crested caracara and falcons. It is quite rare today to find the short-eared owl and there also are black-chinned siskins. Common English sparrows can be seen near the ranch houses. The starling is one of the loveliest birds on the islands and there also are austral blackbirds and canaries.

The Malvinas had a native mammal which unfortunately today is extinct. We refer to the wolf-fox of the Malvinas, where he was called warrahs; it looked half way in between a wolf and a fox, shorter than the first one because it had shorter legs but it was stockier. The tail was longer and bushier than the wolf's.

Towards 1850 it was hunted relentlessly because of the damage it caused in sheep flocks and the last wolf-fox must have been killed in the Malvinas around 1873.

All the animals which have been mentioned, even the ones which are now extinct, existed in the Malvinas at the time of Spanish domain, that is until 1811. Only some species like the warrah have disappeared.

Tussock grass is almost two meters high, there is plenty of white grass, diddle dee, sphagnums, a moss that turns into peat with the passing of time.

The balsam bog forms large, hard, rounded humps.

Veronica is a very attractive bush with yellow odorous flowers.

There are also pale maidens, with white flowers, and wild celery.

CHAPTER IV

Discovery and History of the Malvinas up to 1763

The theories and studies on the possible discoverers of the islands cover a century, the XVIth century, and include the following sailors and expeditions:

1) Amerigo Vespucci, in his controversial voyage of 1501/1502 with a Portuguese expedition.
2) The French sailor Binot Palmier de Gonneville in his voyage of 1503/1504.
3) Magellan's expedition in 1520.
4) Esteban Gomez, Portuguese pilot, who was a deserter from Magellan's expedition, in 1520.
5) Captain Pedro de Vera in his ship "Anunciada" from the expedition of Friar Garcia Jofre de Loaysa, in 1526.
6) The ship "San Pedro" of Alcazaba's expedition in the first days of 1536.
7) The ship "Incognita" of the Bishop of Plasencia's expedition, also known as Alonso de Camargo's expedition, really led by Friar Francisco de la Ribera, in 1540.
8) The English captain John Davis in command of the ship "Desire", in 1592.
9) The English captain Ricard Hawkins, in 1594.
10) The Dutchman Sebald de Weert, in command of the "Geloof" (The Faith), on the 24th of January 1600. Usually accepted, without argument, either as discoverer or rediscoverer.

The discovery of the Malvinas is a difficult historical subject because it requires a specialized knowledge of several disciplines and specialized subjects of maritime history.

Firstly, we should be acquainted with all the existing bibliography and documents on the discovery, the geographical aspects covering physical aspects, meteorology, ocean currents, the ice pack, temperatures, visibility, mist, fogs, marine and terrestrial flora and fauna; also with ships and naval knowledge of the period, also the instruments and the precision of the instruments used to calculate locations at sea and on land.

Sailing ships and caravels would lay to and lower sails in storms and would try to lose the least course. The calculations of longitude by difference in time with the meridian of origin was very erroneous as time was measured with little precision by hour-glasses. Mistakes of several degrees of longitude could be made, representing 100 or 200 miles of error. The distances sailed were also estimated and could be grossly incorrect, by from 10 to 30 percent, produced not only by human errors, but by the action of winds and currents.

Meteorology and cartography are two other very important sciences.

Of the list of possible discoverers of the islands mentioned at the beginning of the chapter, we can discard four as being very improbable or directly discardable: Binot Palmier de Gonneville, Captain Pedro de Vera with his ship "Anunciada", the Friar Garcia de Loayza expedition of 1526, the ship "San Pedro" of Alcazaba's 1535 expedition.

1) *Amerigo Vespucci* has been named discoverer of the Malvinas during the famous voyage of 1501/1502 which has aroused so much controversy. About Vespucci, it has been questioned whether he really was the author of his famous "letters" or "narrations", if he really made some of his journeys, if he discovered the Rio de la Plata, if he reached "Cananor" in the latitudes of 50°S. of the Patagonian coast and whether he discovered the Malvinas or not.

It is not easy to unravel the truth when a large experience is required in navigation and the cartography of the period and it would be difficult to follow the reasoning of passionate devotees, who sometimes add very questionable deductions to truths or half-truths.

We shall not enter deeply into an argument in which illustrious persons or people who were well equipped with arguments and knowledge have participated. We shall only say that, for us, Amerigo Vespucci was a noteworthy astronomer and cosmographer, who deserved the high opinion which Christopher Columbus held of him, and also deserved the honour of being nominated "Master Pilot" by the Spanish Court.

What interests us is his third voyage which started on the 10th or the 13th of May 1501 in Lisbon. It was a Portuguese expedition under the command of Gonzalo Coelho and which reached the Brazilian coast at 5°S. and from there followed the coast to 25°S. or 32°S. As from there, Vespucci took over command —a strange event explained by the fact that, because of the Tordesillas Treaty, they would, at that point, enter into the zone belonging to the King of Spain.

It is about from this point on the coast where Vespucci took over command, that the most complicated discussions take place. According to some historians, Vespucci continued to follow the coastline until

50°S. This opinion is shared in our country by Dr. Roberto Levillier, Ingeniero Nicanor Alurralde and Dr. Enrique de Gandia. They base themselves, above all, on interpretations of the Vespucci letter "Mundus Novus" of 1502 (of which many translations have been made into Latin, German, French and Italian) and on another letter named "from Lisbon", of the same year.

Another group of historians refute the opinions of the above, giving a different interpretation to the "Mundus Novus" and base themselves on a letter named "Lettera" of 1504, which is Vespucci's most extensive and detailed letter and which expresses that, from the coast of Brazil, he followed the course of the Sirocco wind (that is to say towards the S.E.), covering 500 leagues by sea down to latitude 50°S. (in some narrations 52° South).

We should point out that Dr. Roberto Levillier, author of "America, the Well Named" (a work in two volumes of "Mundus Novus" and "Amerigo Vespucci") and a passionate "Vespucista" has given a large supply of information, some of it questionable, in support of the theory that Vespucci sailed the South American coastline down to 50°S.

A great part of his thesis is based on numerous charts which show a River Jordan, which would be the Rio de la Plata, as it was at the same latitude as Needles Cape in Africa (35°S.). Also because the river Cananor would be close to the 50°S latitude and it would be for this reason that it has retained the name of Bay of Camarones.

Dr. Levillier's postulations based on charts have been dealt a rude blow by the studies of Vice-Admiral Ernesto Basilico in his work "The Third Voyage of Amerigo Vespucci" and by those of Lt. Commander Roberto Barreiro Meiro of Spain. They have proven, almost simultaneously, the inexactitudes in correlating well known parts of Africa and South America in maps subsequent to Vespucci's voyage. The South American parts appear more elongated to the south the higher the latitude, so that there is no correlation between Needles Cape in South Africa and the Rio Jordan, which is some 23° S and not 35°. In the same way, Cananor is no more than 24° S. These two works, in my opinion, are very novel and convincing, and would demonstrate that Vespucci did reach 50°S. on our Patagonian coast.

Some few authors, supporters of the voyage along our coast theory, make him appear as discoverer of the Rio de la Plata and the Patagonian coast, and they depict him also as discoverer of the Malvinas. Louis Antoine de Bougainville, colonizer of the Malvinas, was of this opinion, and so are Ingeniero Nicanor Alurralde and Dr. Enrique de Gandia. The savant Alexander Humboldt believed it could be Patagonia; A. Varnaghen believed that it could be San Pedro island of the South Georgias, which fits better to Vespucci's description; Admiral Pedro Casal supposed it was a giant tubular iceberg. Lastly, Vice-Admiral Ernesto Basilico refutes the discovery of the Malvinas by Vespucci.

Let us see how the discovery was made by Vespucci, according to his famous "Lettera"; "and we sailed so much with this wind (the "Sirocco), that we found ourselves in latitudes so high that the midday "fix was 52° above the horizon and we could no longer see the stars of "the Little Bear nor of the Big Bear constellations, being distant some "500 leagues from the port we sailed from due to the Sirocco (S.E.). "This was the 3rd of April 1502. That day a storm blew up so strong "that it made us furl all our sails and run with bare masts with strong "winds that blew from the South-East, with enormous waves and stormy "gusts, and such was the tempest that all the fleet was greatly fearful. "The nights were very long and we had one, on the 7th of April that "was of fifteen hours, duration, since the sun was at the end of Aries "and in this region it was winter, as Your Majesty can calculate.

"In the middle of this storm, on the 7th April, we sighted a new "land, which we sailed alongside of for almost 20 leagues, finding the "coast wild, and we did not see any harbour or people, I believe because "the cold was so intense that none of us could remedy it or bear it".

As we can see, this description does not correspond to the Malvinas, full of harbours, whose coasts are not "wild" and who do not have any island 20 leagues (118 kilometres) long. It fits the Georgias better, or a giant tubular iceberg, seen in the middle of a frightful storm. Nor is so cold a climate normal in the Malvinas, we are told.

Let us say then that Vespucci, of whom it is debated whether he sailed our coasts or headed towards the open sea, whether he did discover or not the Río de la Plata and the Patagonian coast, the Malvinas, the South Georgias or an iceberg, did describe an island in terms which do not correspond to the Malvinas. Only the latitude, 50°S. or 52°S. would be correct.

Therefore we believe it very improbable that Vespucci discovered the Malvinas.

2) *The Magellan Expedition of 1520.* Several authors attribute the discovery of the Malvinas to the Magellan Expedition. This assumption is based on the cartography inmediately subsequent to the expedition; but nothing is mentioned of such a discovery in the famous Diaries of Antonio de Pigafeta, the Piloto Albo, nor in what is related by Maximiliano de Taancilvano, which càn be found in the "Collection of Documents" in Navarrete's and other editions. They are the only complete and contemporary accounts of the voyage.

The discovery could have been made by a ship which Magellan sent out to carry out explorations, or which was carried close to the strait by some strong wind. Bearing in mind that a ship in these circumstances would be absent for several days or even weeks, and that after discovering the islands no record is made of the fact — all this does not seem very probable. But it could be that neither Albo nor Pigafeta were on board the ship, or, even stranger still, were on board but did not record the fact.

The cartography, on the other hand, seems to support the discovery thesis.

In Diego de Ribero's charts of 1529, a group of islands appears which are named "Sanson". They are 8 or 9 islands which could be the Malvinas. Others which are called "de los Patos" are very close to the coast. The Sanson islands are quite a lot further North (49° S.) than the Malvinas (51° S.) and a little more than half the distance to the coast.

Another very interesting chart is one published by Professor Manuel Destombes in 1938 and which was in the Top Kapi Sarayi in Istambul, and which was later taken to the Aghalar Mosque in the same city.

In that chart, which has been dated 1522/23, only the North coast of the Magellan Strait appears, and to the East of the mouth of the Strait, at some 56 leagues (180 miles) another enormous island can be seen, almost 300 miles in length. The Malvinas are almost due East (85°) of the mouth ot the Magellan Strait and some 81 leagues, (of 5,920 metres each) away. The fact that it appears as a large island detracts somewhat from the value of the assumption.

In later charts found in "The Santa Cruz Compendium of the Islands", Juan Bautista Agnese 1543/45, Martinez 1577 and Olives 1580 also included the "Sanson" islands, among others. They always appear situated well to the North and close to the coast.

The fact that the Malvinas have been shown close to the coast may be attributed to erroneous estimations of longitude — very normal ir the XVIth Century, or to deliberately moving them toward the West to "ensure that they fall" within the Spanish zone of the Treaty of Tordesillas. The Spanish moved islands and coasts to the West and the Portuguese did the same, but towards the East.

Consequently, although faithful, documented accounts of the discovery are lacking, the cartography shows that the discovery of the Malvinas by some of the ships of Magellan's Expedition is very probable.

3) *Esteban Gomez.* On the 1st of November 1520 he deserted from the Straits with the ship "San Antonio" and arrived in Spain, where he was submitted to an enquiry on the 6th of May 1521. Ratto has supposed that Gomez, on leaving the Straits bound for the Cape of Good Hope, discovered the Malvinas. This is not so; the documents of the hearings show that he did not set sail for the Cape but for the Guineas, on the African coast, sailing directly to Spain and reaching Seville on the 6th of May 1521. Thus he did not pass close to the Malvinas. Neither is anything said about the discovery of the islands in the testimony given by 53 members of his crew during the hearings.

What we have expounded proves almost without doubt that Esteban Gomez did not discover the islands on his return voyage to Spain;

but he may well have been the first to broadcast the discovery by one of Magellan's ships.

Esteban Gomez, who made other voyages, met Diego de Ribero in la Coruña. Diego de Ribero was the cartographer who in 1529 drew the map where the Sanson islands are shown. Proof of this is established by a document from the "Indies Archives" which shows that when Gomez returned from America in 1525, he gave Diego de Rivera an Indian interpreter, whose name was also Diego. (Lists of Happenings to certain Indians — General Archive of the Indies — Account 427 N° 2).

This would show that Diego de Ribero received news of the voyage of Magellan as far as the entrance to the Straits, from a good source. Later he was to complete his map, on the return of the "Victoria" to Spain.

4) *Discovery by the "Incognita" in 1540.* The discovery of the Malvinas Islands by the ship "Incognita" forming part of the Bishop of Plasencia's Expedition on the 4th of February 1540 is very probable.

This expedition which sailed from Seville on the 12th of January 1540, lost its flag-ship in the Straits of Magellan. Another of the ships, whose log we possess, managed to make land, after riding out a storm which had blown it out of the Straits, where the crew remained for 10 months. Of this ship, neither its name nor the name of its captain is known. This is why it is called "Incógnita".

This possible discovery has been dealt with very well by Julius Goebel (Jr.) in his classic book "The Struggle of the Falklands Islands" and by Vice-Admiral Ernesto Basilico, so often mentioned here, in his work "The Fleet of the Bishop of Plasencia and the Discovery of the Malvinas".

Two versions of this voyage exist, one is of the ship "Incognita" and the second is of one of the other ships that were left after the flag-ship sunk.

From the first narrative (of the ship "Incognita"), one learns that on the 20th of January 1540 the fleet entered the mouth of the Straits and on the 22nd lost the flag-ship. The other two ships are not mentioned because they had separated. The "Incognita" tried to save the shipwrecked crew, but the storm did not permit this. On the 27th she tried again to enter the mouth of the Straits, but without success. Again, on the 29th of January she was unsuccessful and on the 31st of January, while at anchor, a strong S.S.E. wind rose and she broke her anchor cable and was forced to tack windward.

The log is interrupted here and on the 4th of February they sighted land (in other words, they had been sailing the open seas and eight or nine islands appeared "which are on the chart" (believing them to the "Sansons").

They stayed on "these islands in a large Bay called "de las Zorras" (of the Foxes) until the 3rd December 1540, that is to say, for ten months, after which they sailed with good weather from the South and South-East and went round the island where they "lost their small cannons and the the wind changed to South-West" and "they ran two days with it to look for the land from the North". On the 5th they were at fortynine and one sixth degrees of latitude, which is to say, some 70 or 75 miles to the north of the Malvinas.

The second narrative relates that one of the ships arrived from the expedition which had been in the island of Santo Tome and had encountered one of the four ships of the Bishop of Plasencia's expedition there. On board were two men from the "Incognita" who related something similar to the previous version.

Summing up, Dr. Julius Goebel (Jr.) and Admiral Basilico coincide in affirming that the ship "Incognita" had reached the Malvinas, but Commander Hector R. Ratto affirms that the "Incognita" had reached the Beagle Channel which also has bays and islands.

Admiral Basilico's version convincingly demonstrates that the islands are the Malvinas for the following reasons:

1) That as from the 31st of January 1540 according to the first version, the "Incognita", while anchored, was struck by a violent storm from the South South-East which snapped the anchor cable and she was carried dangerously close to land. A lull followed and the ship was carried out of the Straits. The wind had to be West or South-West since a Northwest wind would have permitted them to have remained in the Straits, being sheltered. The narrative is interrupted for four days and on the 4th of February, in the morning, they sighted "eight or nine islands, which are on the chart".
They continue relating their course through the islands which they describe, coinciding thus with the Malvinas (clean channels and many bays) even though they talk of very high mountains.
Admiral Basilico concludes that the wind and the currents carried them toward the East North-East and they had to believe that the islands were the Sansons of the Diego Ribeiro chart.

2) That the wind was West South-West because they ran without being able to return to the Straits and that the large bay was that of San Julian in the Malvinas, which is closed and in a labyrinth of islands, where they ran aground.

3) That they called the harbour where they ran aground "Port of the Foxes", "because there were many of them". That the foxes, or wolf-foxes of the Malvinas were abundant in the islands, where they were known by the name of "Warrah".

4) That the account says that the land appeared to be a headland of the

terra firma that ran to the South of the Strait (the "Terra Incognita Australis") and lies East to West referred to the mouth of the Straits. This indicates without doubt that they were in the Malvinas.

5) That mention is made of wood that comes out of the Straits and consists of trunks carried from the Strait by the current from the Southwest to the Northeast (of the Malvinas). Savants and sailors who visited the Malvinas mentioned this, and even today there is a Firewood Cove there. Also, they found a piece of planking which came from the Straits where the flagship was lost. This reference is very important and continues to point out that "all this land is flat, without a single tree, very windy and too cold, because eight months of the year it always snows" and the winds are South-West or West or North-West, which fits in exactly with the Malvinas. They also inform of very solid turf, whose layer is between two and ten feet thick, which occurs in the Malvinas.

The vegetation described corresponds to the Malvinas "tussocks" and other bushes, the fauna corresponds to land and sea geese and seals. The quantity of islands, the climate and the duration of summer and winter also fits the description of the Malvinas.

6) That the narrative reports that they sailed on the 24th of November and on the 3rd of December 1540 left the Malvinas with a South and South-East wind, and that on the 5th, i.e., two days later, took a fix on the sun "in forty-nine degrees and a sixth (49° 10' S.). The expression "ran two days to look for Terra Firma of the Northern Part" clearly refers to the northern part of the Magellan Straits, as opposed to "Terra Australis" which for them was Terra Firma of the South (see Antonio de Santa Cruz's chart). This position would be perfectly normal after running with a South-west wind for 180 miles from the Malvinas with a velocity of 3.7 knots.

Vice-admiral Basilico continues with the second narrative according to what two of the "Incognita" crew relate, taken from a letter written to Lazaro Aleman from Lisbon dated the 19th July 1541, in which is said, very briefly, that the "Incognita" was carried "toward the Spanish part and entered a bay of more than sixty leagues where they remained ten months". It means that they entered a bay after sixty leagues. Apart from an obscure phrase of "they took the coast below", the rest coincides with the first narrative, in general, regarding the description of the islands. The "coast below", supposedly, is the southern side of the Straits.

Dr. Julius Goebel (Jr.) also agrees that the "Incognita" reached the Malvinas where she remained those months before returning to Spain.

All is so logical, clear and convincing, that one can not do less than agree with the deductions of Admiral Basilico. Nevertheless, Commander Hector R. Ratto, in his book "Bordejeando" published in the Bulletin of the Centro Naval in 1927, expressed the opinion that the "Incognita" passed through the Straits of Le Maire and reached the Beagle.

Admiral Basilico pointed out several errors in that work, which was one of Commander Ratto's first, and when that great historian supposes that a wind from the Northwest would throw them out to sea, pointed out that with such a wind, they could have remained in the Straits. He also states that coming from the North you cannot see the Isla de los Estados for the N.N.E. and that the phrase "they see the islands that are in the chart" can only refer to the Sansons, which are much further North. He then shows how doubtful it would have been to enter Flinders Bay, as Ratto states, and clearly indicates errors of interpretation and also some assumptions which are not correct. He is also of the opinion that the "eight or nine islands" which were sighted cannot refer to Tierra del Fuego, as Ratto says.

In the light of a comment about burnt grass in the Malvinas, which for Ratto was not possible as there were no inhabitants, Admiral Basilico pointed out that the origin of the fire could have been lightning.

We shall add that it would be impossible, being in the Beagle, from its Eastern mouth to Port Almanza, not to see Alacalufe or Yamana Indians during the ten months they spent ashore. The Malvinas were a group of islands without inhabitants. On the other hand we believe that close to Port Almanza (Port of the Foxes according to Ratto) there were trees.

Consequently, for us, the ideas stated by Goebel (Jr.) and more extensively and clearly by Vice-admiral Ernesto Basilico are perfectly valid, and we agree that the "Incognita" went to the Malvinas.

We shall now go on to "The Compendium of the Islands" of Alonso de Santa Cruz, published in 1908 by Franz R. von Wiesser, in Innsbruck, based on two Codexes which are in the Imperial Library in Vienna.

Alonso de Santa Cruz prepared a narration which is known as "The Compendium of the Islands of Alonso de Santa Cruz", published in 1541, one year after the voyage of the Bishop of Plasencia's expedition, and when reporting on information which he states came from said expedition he said: "Having passed the Cape of the Straits, we ran "down the coast again toward the South-East until we enter a large bay "for about fifty leagues and from the bay we run back up the Northeast "for abouth fifty, up to a cape which is next to a bay of the Islands, "which is between two capes and in front of which are two rias. All the "coast is full of large and small bays, which was also discovered by the "Bishop of Plasencia's fleet, as we said before; the said Cape is sixty "leagues to the Northeast of the mouth of the Straits, after which much "of the coast runs to the Southeast".

As Julius Goebel (Jr.) says, it does not clarify if this was discovered by the "Incognita", but we note that the description refers to the islands being off a terra firma which the cartographer read as "Terra Australis". Furthermore, it mentions the fleet of the Bishop of Plasencia as the source of the information about the area. The information about the cape, the islands and the Bay of the Foxes cannot be from any other source but the "Incognita".

One can see on the chart a large bay that starts at the mouth of the Magellan Straits lying in "Terra Australis Incognita" and has a cape with two points on its extreme right and a bay in the centre. This bay is without doubt the Bay of Foxes and two small islands go with it. The cape, the bay with the two islands are without any doubt the Malvinas joined to the "Terra Australis Incognita", since the crewmen of the "Incognita" assumed that what lay to the South was "terra firma". In the chart the distance from the mouth of the Straits to the Cape and the islands is only 56 or 58 leagues and within latitudes 50° and 51° S.

If we bear in mind all this, we must agree that Vice-admiral Ernesto Basilico's theory is plainly justified, namely that the cape with two points with the bay in the middle and the two islands, corresponds to the Malvinas Islands.

In "The Compendium of the Islands" of Alonso de Santa Cruz, the islands and the cape which represent the Malvinas are, from the centre of the mouth of the Magellan Straits, within the azimuths 076° and 085° (from North to East). If the declination had not been taken into account, that is, if they were only magnetic azimuths, then the declination as calculated approximately for the year 1540 would have to be added, which would be equal to 7° E. and then the values would be 083° and 092° respectively.

As for the distance, the narrative says it is 60 leagues, but in the chart it is a bit less, 58 leagues (191.8 miles or 184.4 miles if we take the league of 5,920 metres).

The real location of the islands, measured from the east mouth of the Straits of Magellan is 81 leagues between 073° and 089°.

The location of the islands, as shown in "The Compendium of the Islands" is quite acceptable in azimuths and very acceptable in distance.

As a consequence, the discovery of the Malvinas by the "Incognita" is indisputably certain. We accept it, but we recognize that some points of the argument may be dissented with or refuted.

5) *Landing by John Davis.* The English assume that the great English mariner John Davis discovered the islands in the ship "Desire" on the 14th of August 1592.

John Davis was either a deserter or had left the corsair expedition

of John Cavendish and had "on the 14th of August 1592 discovered
"certain islands, carried there by a storm, islands never discovered
"before, and to which no known account makes mention, which lie
"some 50 leagues or more from the coast to the East and lie Northerly
"from the Straits".

This version is very similar to that presented in "The Compendium
of the Islands" of Santa Cruz in 1541, in azimuth and in distance.

In consequence, the discovery by John Davis seems doubtful for
the following reasons:

1) The account of his voyage and discovery was published by John
Jane, one of his crew, eight years later, in 1600. In that year, on the
14th of July, Sebald de Weert had returned to Holland, although, at
present, we do not intend to link these facts. John Jane's account
suffers from fantasy in other passages.

2) He was a deserter who had to discover something to improve his
personal situation in England on his return.

3) The siting of the islands is inexact even for that period, for a great
mariner like John Davis. The islands are not described.

4) He could have sighted tubular icebergs or low clouds.

5) The chart from the famous "Hakluyt" collection of English voyages
shows the Sanson Islands and not those that Davis had discovered.

6) The English version is suspiciously similar to that of "The Compendium of the Islands" of Santa Cruz of 1541. Let us then say that
this description presents more points of unreliability than the one of
the "Incognita".

Let us then look at the English version of the supposed discovery
by John Davis: "The ninth had a sore storme, so that wee were
"constrained to hull, for our sailes were not to indure any force. The 14
"wee were driven in among certain Isles never before discovered by any
"known relation lying fiftie leagues or better from the shoare East and
"northerly from the Streight: in which place unlesse it had pleased God
"of his wonderful mercie to have ceased the wind wee must of necessitie
"have perished. But the wind shifting to the East Wee directed our
"course for the Streights, and the 18 of August wee fell with the Cape
"in a very thick fogge and the same night wee andkered ten leagues
"within the Cape. The 19th day wee passed the first and the second
"Streights". These excepts have been taken out of the old English text
found in Julius Goebel (Jr.)'s book published by New Haven and
London in 1927.

This same paragraph was translated into Spanish and published in a book called "La Pugna por las Islas Malvinas" edited by Abaco, in Buenos Aires, in 1950. But the translation was poor in parts.

In the book "The Seamen's Secrets" published by the same John Davis in 1594, a wind rose is shown, where the winds are separated by quarters (11° 15') between the Northeast (045°) and the East (090°).

There are three bearings, firstly N.E. by East (056° 15'), then E.N.E. (067° 30') and finally East by North (078° 45'), between North-East and East. The expression East and Northerly could be E.N.E. (067° 30') or East by North (078° 45'). Davis's islands could be between these azimuths. If they were magnetic azimuths excluding the declination, a correction of 14° E. would have to be made, giving true azimuths of 081° 31' and 092° 45'.

The distance "50 leagues or more" brings the uncertainty of the league used, if it were the English league of the XVIIth Century of 20 leagues per degree or the Spanish one of 5,920 metres per degree. In the first case it would be 139 present day miles, and in the second case it would be 160 miles.

We can see that Davis's "certain isles" are in almost the same azimuth as those discovered by the "Incognita" and only 10 leagues different in distance. The location of the isles "discovered" by Davis is fairly acceptable.

Nevertheless the suspicion that this "discovery" was concocted by John Jane to improve Davis's delicate position as a deserter and that he based it on the Spanish discoveries is strengthened by the following similar suspicion:

The version of the islands found by the "Incognita" according to Alonso de Santa Cruz, is the following: the cape mentioned (that of the Malvinas configuration) is sixty leagues to the East North East of the mouth of the Straits.

The text of John Jane, translated into Spanish, says "certain islands. . . lie 50 leagues or more from the coast East and northerly from the Straits".

In the chart of "The Compendium of the Islands", we have measured 58 leagues instead of what the text indicates, but if one measures from the North coast of the Straits, or near it, it is between 58 and 54 leagues. Therefore, if the position of the islands should be given in the English version, the most correct would be "50 leagues or more".

As for the azimuth "East and Northerly" which translates as "este y nortemente" or also by "Este-noreste" (East Northeast), it is suspiciously similar to the spanish text of "The Compendium of the Islands" "es-nordeste" (East-Northeast).

The English version of Goebel translates it as "East-Northeast". One can suppose that "East and Northerly" is a bad translation of the Original Spanish (East-Northeast).

The English version of Davis's discovery is then very suspiciously similar to that of "The Compendium of the Islands" of Santa Cruz.

All this, plus the reasons previously stated, make the discovery of the Malvinas Islands by John Davis doubtful.

Even if we consider it in the most benevolent way possible, it must be borne in mind that if Davis did discover the Malvinas, the ship "Incognita" did it better since its location is as correct as that of the English discovery and the distance more closely approximates to the real distance.

6) *The possible discovery of the islands by Richard Hawkins — 2nd of February 1594.* This discovery has merited great attention by Argentine and foreign authors; but all of them emphasize the differences between the description and the reality of the islands, and the inexactitude of the reference to the latitude, which is stated as "approximately at 48° S.".

As a consequence, the discovery of the Malvinas islands by Richard Hawkins is very improbable.

7) *Discovery by Sebald de Weert — 24th January 1600.* This is generally accepted without objections as the first sighting and is reflected in the subsequent cartography. It is considered that if Sebald de Weert discovered the Sebaldine Islands (Jason Islands for the English), then he logically discovered the Malvinas.

In the year 1598, five ships sailed from Texel (Holland) under the orders of Admiral Jacob Mahu and one of them was commanded by Sebald de Weert. The voyage began with bad luck because Mahu died in Atlantic waters and the command had to be taken over by Simon de Cordes. They arrived at San Julian on the 3rd of April 1599 and after entering the Straits of Magellan anchored close to the islands called Isabel and Santa Magdalena. On entering the Pacific, a strong storm separated two of the ships from the rest, and they returned to the Straits. One of these, the "Geloof" (The Faith) was under the command of Sebald de Weert. This mariner, with his ship, reached the Atlantic Ocean again (the other ship had returned to the Pacific) on the 22nd of January 1600 and set sail for Europe, but on the 24th, in latitude 50°40' discovered three islands which he named "Sebaldines" and which are also known as the Jason islands, in the Malvinas archipelago.

The position given by Sebald de Weert indicated a latitude of 50°40' and 60 leagues from the coast.

This distance is given in possibly Dutch leagues which were 15 per degree, making an equivalent of 70 Spanish leagues. In any case the distance is within ten to twenty leagues of the real one. Furthermore, Sebald de Weert published a sketch that corresponds with reality.

Sebald de Weert is generally accepted then as "the discoverer of the Malvinas" or re-discoverer, since we consider that the first discovery was made by the ship "Incognita" of the Bishop of Plasencia's expedition.

The "Geloof" arrived in Holland on the 14th of July 1600 and since then the Sebaldines figure in the charts with fair exactitude.

As a summary of all the above, we consider that there are insufficient arguments to attribute the discovery to Vespucci, Esteban Gomez, Pedro de Vera of Loaysa's expedition, Alcazaba, or Richard Hawkins. The arguments in favour of Magellan's expedition or the one by John Davis are doubtful.

For us, the cases which appear the most substantiated are those of the "Incognita" in spite of its difficult and confused argumentation and that of Sebald de Weert.

We consider the suspicion well founded that, in the account of John Davis's expedition, John Jane fabricated the discovery of "certain islands" so as to enhance the image of his captain, branded as a deserter, and to do this, he based himself on "The Compendium of the Islands" by Alonso de Santa Cruz of 1541.

A ship called "Geloof" (the Faith), under the command of Sebald de Weert, which had formed part of a Dutch expedition which sailed from Texel in 1598, upon returning from the Straits of Magellan, discovered two small islands on the 24th of January 1600. He located them and described them. There is no doubt that they are the Sebaldines (Jasons for the English) which form part of the Malvinas archipelago.

In summary, Sebald de Weert is generally accepted as discoverer of the Malvinas and the Spanish ship "Incognita", which had done so before, had carried out the pre-discovery.

8) *The period from 1600 to 1764.*   In this period, the islands were sighted and even visited by Dutch, English and French sailors.

In 1616, the Dutch expedition of Schouten and Le Maire sighted the islands on the 18th of January.

On the 8th of January 1683, an English ship under the command of buccaneer John Cook, with the explorer-corsair-naturalist William Dampier on board, gave a good siting of the islands.

Captain John Strong, with the ship "Welfare" (or "Farewell") left Plymouth on a commercial voyage on the 11th of November 1689 and sighted the Malvinas on the 27th of January 1690, discovering the channel which separates the two main islands. He called it Falkland, probably in honour of Viscount Falkland (1659—1694) who was Commissioner of the English Admiralty. He called the islands Hawkins Land.

As from 1698 the French from Saint Malo initiated a second period of sightings and discoveries in the Malvinas, which were to take their name from these celebrated sailors from Brittany, in the English

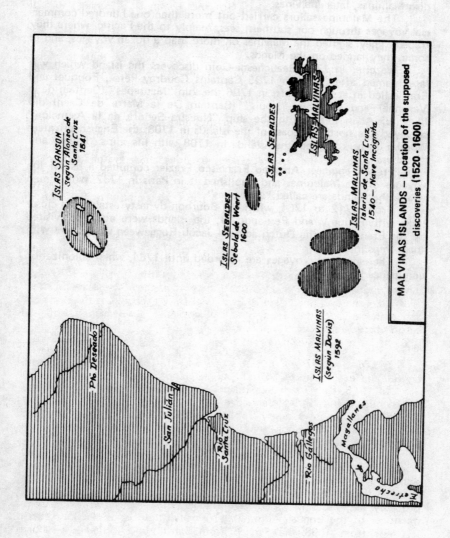

ISLAS SANSON
Segun Alonso de
Santa Cruz
1541

ISLAS SEBALDES
Sebald de Weert
1600

ISLAS SEBALDES

ISLAS MALVINAS

ISLAS MALVINAS
Islario de Santa Cruz
1540 - Nave Incognita

ISLAS MALVINAS
(Segun Davis)
1592

Pto Deseado

San Julián

Rio Santa Cruz

Rio Gallegos

Magallanes

Maire

MALVINAS ISLANDS — Location of the supposed
discoveries (1520 - 1600)

Channel. The islands were called "Iles Malouines" and thence the Spanish Maluinas, later Malvinas.

The Malouine sailors carried out more than one hundred commercial voyages through our southern seas, mainly to the Pacific, where they traded. They sighted the Malvinas on more than a dozen voyages, and in some, they landed on the islands.

We cite: in 1701 Beauchesne-Goin discovers the island which was later named after him; in 1705 Captains Coudray Perée, Fouquet and Eran called in at the islands; in 1706 the ship "Maurepas" (Captain de la Verunne) and the ship "Louis" (Captain De la Marre de Caen) did likewise; Alain Peree with the ship "Nuestra Señora de la Asunción" surveyed the northern coast of the islands in 1708; the English privateer Woodes Rogers sighted the islands in 1708 with his ships "Duke" and "Duchess".

French engineer Amadeo Francisco Frezier compiled a list of the voyages of the Malouines and published it in Paris in 1732, with a map where the islands are called "Nouvelles".

From 1712 to 1764, when the Bourbon dynasty established closer links with Felipe V and Fernando VI, the islands were no longer visited by the French, but the Dutch admiral Jacob Roggeween went there with three ships in 1721.

Thereafter, no voyages are recorded until 1764, when colonization commenced.

CHAPTER V

The Malvinas under Spanish rule

The first to try and colonize the Malvinas were the French, determined to recover after the disastrous Peace of Paris of 1763, through which they had lost important possessions.

Louis Antoine de Bougainville, born in Paris in 1729, a diplomat and an outstanding sailor, managed to convince the Duke of Choiseul, Louis XV's War and Naval Minister, to carry out the colonization of the Malvinas.

Bougainville's expedition sailed from Saint-Malo on the 8th September 1763 with the frigate "L'Aigle" and the corvette "Le Sphinx", and after arriving at Montevideo, where they gave to understand that their destination was India, they sailed for the Malvinas, where they arrived on the 31st of January.

On the 2nd of February 1764, the Bougainville expedition entered a wide bay on the north eastern side of the East Malvina Island. The French called it French Bay or East Bay (the Spaniards called it Annunciation Bay and the English called it Berkeley Sound).

In early March 1764, the French built a fort and then a series of buildings, making up a township named Saint Louis. It was inaugurated on the 5th of April of that same year.

England, already determined to intervene in the islands, sent an expedition to establish one or more colonies. The expedition led by Captain John Byron went to the Malvinas and on the 15th January 1765 entered a wide harbour made up of three islands (Trinidad, Vigia and the N.E. part of Gran Malvina) and named it Egmont in honour of the First Lord of the Admiralty, the Second Earl of Egmont.

The English who disembarked there were there only for a short time, they raised their flag and took possession of all the neighbouring islands under the name of "Falkland Islands" for King George III of England. Byron left the islands shortly thereafter. The French had already been living in Port Saint Louis for a year, but the English were unaware of this. The following year, Captain John Macbride landed at Port Egmont with three ships on the 8th January 1766 and established a fort which he called "Fort George".

When Spain learned of the occupation of the Malvinas by the French, she initiated a strong and resolute claim against her French ally King Louis XV. The negotiations were long, but France internationally recognized Spain's right to the islands and resolved to hand them over

Louis Antoine de Bougainville, according to an old print. Reproduction from the book by Julius Goebel (Jr.).

to the Spaniards once the latter had compensated Bougainville for all the expenses which he had privately incurred.

Meanwhile the English had become aware of the French settlement, which they visited, but withdrew, leaving a declaration in which they affirmed that the islands belonged to England.

Spain, as already agreed with Boungainville, decided to pay him 616,108 Tours Pounds, the equivalent of 18 soldiers' pay and 11 gold coins. Of this amount, 200,000 Tours Pounds were to be paid in Paris and the remainder, equivalent to 75,721 and ¾ pesos fuertes, or silver coins weighing one ounce, would be paid in Buenos Aires. Furthermore, Spanish Royal Navy Commander Don Felipe Ruiz Puente was sent out as Governor of the Malvinas, coming under the Governor and Captain General of Buenos Aires.

The brand new Spanish Governor was to sail out with the frigates "Liebre" and "Esmeralda" and was to be joined at Montevideo by the frigate "La Boudeuse" with Bougainville on board.

On the 2nd April 1767 the now Captain Felipe Ruiz Puente took solemn possession of the French colony of Port Saint Louis.

One year later it was re-named Puerto de Nuestra Señora de la Soledad, when an image of the Virgin Mary of that name was enthroned there.

As from the time when the Spanish installed themselves there, every year, in the summer months, the annual provisioning of the colony was carried out. This was made from Montevideo with one or two war frigates at first and later with corvettes or even with brigantines, accompanied by one or more lesser cargo and transport vessels, so as to carry cattle, victuals and stores.

On the 28th November 1769, in the San Carlos Straits, a Spanish ship bound for Puerto Soledad encountered an English ship sailing from Port Egmont. As from that date the Spaniards knew for sure of the presence of the English on the islands, although they did not know where they were located.

Following orders from the Spanish Crown, the Governor of Buenos Aires, Francisco Bucarelli y Urzua, gave strict orders to Captain Juan Ignacio Madariaga on the 26th March 1770, to find and expel the English from the Malvinas.

Firstly, an exploratory frigate was sent out under the command of Commander Fernando Rubalcava, who found the English settlement in Port Egmont and returned informing that there was only one English ship in that port.

On the 11th of May 1770 Madariaga set out with his naval force composed of four frigates: the "Industria" with 28 twelve pounder guns; the "Santa Barbara" with 26 eight pounder guns; the "Santa Catalina" with 26 twelve pounder guns and the "Santa Rosa" with 20 six pounder guns. Also sailing with this division were the man-of-war "Andaluz" with

View of the bay on East Island, the largest of the Malvinas Islands, and its settlement (1764 - 1765).

forty guns and the brig "San Rafael". The grand total comprised 1,400 troops and sailors and 140 guns including a landing battery.

The 3rd of June 1770 Madariaga anchored in Port Egmont and, after exchanging messages of protest with the English for several days, decided to proceed.

The 10th of June 1770 was the day chosen for the attack, while the English were preparing for the defense. At ten o'clock the battle was started, and fire was opened on the English frigate "La Favorita". This was the English frigate which was there. The launches landed and some cannon shots were exchanged between the opponents. The English did it so as to save their honour and then raised the white flag. There were no casualties.

When the news of the fall of Port Egmont reached England, the return of the settlement and complete satisfaction became a question of honour.

France really did not want war, neither did Spain, far less, without French support. Finally Louis XV asked Carlos III to make a sacrifice so as to avoid a war.

Abandoned by France, the Spanish King negotiated with England and in exchange for a so-called "secret promise", by which England, with its honour saved, would evacuate the Malvinas, decided to give up and return Port Egmont.

In a declaration signed on the 22nd of January 1771 by England and Spain it was established that His Catholic Majesty committed himself "to give inmediate orders so that things should be re-established in Gran Malvina in the Port called Egmont in exactly the same state as they were before the 10th of June 1770".

At the same time the Prince of Masserano stated "in the name of the King, his liege, that His Catholic Majesty's committment to restore possession of the port and fort called Egmont to His Britannic Majesty cannot or should not in any way whatsoever affect the question of the prior right to sovereignty over the Malvinas Islands, also called Falklands. In proof thereof, I, the undersigned, Ambassador Extraordinary, have signed herewith".

England had triumphed. Port Egmont was returned on the 16th September 1771.

Meanwhile, the Prince of Masserano, the Spanish Ambassador to London, shortly afterwards, started pressing for the promised English evacuation to begin, but this was slow in happening.

For nearly six years Felipe Ruiz Puente governed in this far flung and inhospitable station and on the 23rd of January 1773, he handed over command to his relief, Infantry Captain Domingo de Chauri.

After many appeals, the English decided to evacuate the Islands. Was she fulfilling the Secret Promise or was it because of the international situation and the imminent uprising of its great American Colony?

Brigadier Don Felipe Ruiz Puente, First Spanish Governor of the Malvinas, from an oil painting in the Madrid National Museum.

On the 20th or the 22nd of May 1774, the English withdrew from Port Egmont, but left a plaque which said, in English, as follows: "Know all nations, that the Falkland Islands, with their port, stores, landing places, natural harbours, bays and pertinent inlets are the exclusive right and property of His Most Sacred Majesty George III, King of Great Britain. In testimony of which this plaque is placed and the colours of His Britannic Majesty are left flying as a sign of possession by S.W. Clayton, Commanding Officer of the Falkland Islands. A.D. 1774".

As of then the usurpation of sovereignty which Port Egmont typified, was discontinued. The English did not return until several decades later, invoking rights which they had never held and had only acquired through a temporary and illegal occupation.

The Spanish flag in Puerto Soledad was, as from then on, the only expression of sovereignty on the Islands. The Islands belonged to Spain. That nation occupied the Malvinas on the 2nd of April 1767, and as from 1774, with the English withdrawal, remained the only owner until the 13th of February 1811.

During this period the world suffered various military and political commotions, from which Great Britain emerged more powerful than ever.

During the war which ended up with the independence of the United States of America, France and Spain were allies of the Americans and England suffered a set-back which she was, however, to recover from completely and even more firmly in the naval battle of Trafalgar on the 21st of October 1805.

In 1788 Carlos III died and was succeeded by Carlos IV, who was insufficiently prepared to govern in such a difficult period, when the French Revolution and later the Spanish American Revolution, greatly damaged Spain and her Empire.

From 1767 until 1811, we repeat, Spain controlled the Malvinas, and during this period twenty governors held office. All were naval officers except for the second one Domingo de Chauri, who belonged to the Army.

On the 5th of January 1774, a new Governor took charge of the Malvinas, Captain Francisco Gil y Lemos, an outstanding sailor who had made many voyages in the waters of Patagonia and the Malvinas. The governors of the Malvinas came under the Governor of Buenos Aires or the Viceroy of the Rio de la Plata.

Each year, in the Port of Montevideo, an expedition was prepared to effect reliefs and provisioning, made up of one or more ships. The voyages lasted twenty to thirty-five days, or even more, due to the frequent storms.

With the establishment of the Viceroyalty of the Rio de la Plata, all the region of South America, endangered by Portuguese and English ambitions, was fortified.

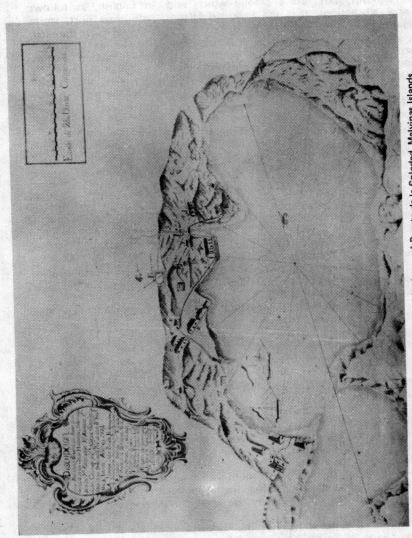

Description of the settlement and harbour of Puerto de la Soledad, Malvinas Islands, prepared by the pilots of the Royal Spanish Navy Don Juan Callejas and Don Narciso Sánchez (1774).

The Naval Station at Montevideo was set up on the 9th of August 1776 and a readied war frigate had to be stationed there to relieve a similar unit stationed at the Malvinas. As time went by and the second period of Spanish naval decline became more marked, the frigates were replaced by corvettes and later on by brigs and even by coastal schooners.

The governors of the Islands had orders to inspect Port Egmont annually so as to verify that the English had not settled there again. In actual fact, English, and also American, sealers and whalers were to be found in the inslands and bays, persistently plundering the fauna in the coasts and harbours of the Malvinas.

The Island was was used as a penitentiary by the Spaniards and always held thirty or more convicts during the greater part of the Spanish period. In the time of Governor Altolaguirre (1781—1783) there were more than forty convicts; many of them were "criollo" farm-hands who worked with the horses and cattle.

Captain Gil y Lemos continued furthering his career in Spain, reaching the rank of Naval Lieutenant-General and he was also appointed Viceroy of Peru. In 1805 he was made Interim Naval Secretary of State and promoted to Admiral rank and was confirmed as Minister in 1806. He died in 1809.

Along with the change of governors used to come the changes of the two chaplains, who until then, were Franciscans.

Inspections of Port Egmont continued and a census was made of cattle, showing a total of 395 head, which grazed in fenced-in grasslands or around Puerto Soledad.

The Naval Lieutenant Don Ramon Carassa, who succeeded Gil y Lemos, was replaced on the 22nd of November 1779 by equal ranking Don Salvador Medina.

In 1780 the penitentiary was established in the Malvinas. At that time the population of the Malvinas was composed of officers, troops, seamen and convicts. Supply ships, brigs or mercantile frigates came annually in the summer with reliefs and stores. The governors of the Malvinas were distinguished officers who subsequently made brilliant careers.

If the price to the Viceroyalty of maintaining Puerto Soledad was high, it is certain that it guaranteed Spanish sovereignty over the Islands.

The civilian population had been evacuated, and no French families or civilian colonizers remained. In the library run by the Fathers of the Franciscan and De La Merced Orders seventeen books could be found, covering such subjects as prayer and morals.

The summer ship helped to make life better for the sailors, soldiers, professionals and convicts which inhabited Puerto Soledad.

Navy Lieutenant Jacinto de Altolaguirre was the first governor of "criollo" origin to take command of the Malvinas. He was born in Buenos Aires on the 15th of July 1754 and was the son of Martin

Altolaguirre, a Spaniard and Doña María Josefa Pando, a native of Buenos Aires.

The family of Jacinto Altolaguirre was large and distinguished and played an important role in both the Colonial and the Post-Independence periods.

The military career of the young Buenos Aires born man started in the Army and he managed to achieve the difficult feat of transferring to the Royal Spanish Navy, where he saw active service in actions against the Berbers in North Africa.

On the 16th of May 1776 he was promoted to Ensign and on the 14th of May 1779 to Lieutenant Junior Grade, serving in the Montevideo Naval Station.

In mid-1780, the industrious Viceroy Vertiz decided to reduce the forces in the Malvinas, and upon following his orders, a large saving was obtained, lowering expeditures to 11,102 pesos, which represented one fifth of what they used to be.

Upon being named Governor, Jacinto Altolaguirre moved to the Islands, arriving there at the beginning of 1781.

At that time the buildings which could be found at Puerto Soledad, the only inhabited place of the Islands, were as follows:

One house for the Governor (built of stone)
One house, for the Port Captain.
One hospital.
Four houses for officers.
One chapel
One barracks for seamen.
One barracks for convicts and troops.
One pier house.
One kiln.
Five rooms for workmen.
One carpenter's shop.
One smithy.
One farm house.
One small house.
One store.
One store, built of stone (for general food items
    and other purposes).
One lookout

all of which total twenty or twenty-five buildings, half of stone and half of blocks of Malvinas turf.

At the time of taking over, Altolaguirre pointed out that the ship's crew should include two carpenters and two caulkers, whereas there was only one of each.

The artillery was divided into three batteries, namely:

1) *San Carlos Battery:* With four eight pounder and two six pounder guns with 972 eight pound rounds and 167 six pound rounds.

2) *Santiago Battery:* With four twenty-four pounders and 1,178 rounds.

3) *San Felipe Baterry:* with three eight pounders and 735 eight pound rounds.

At the head of the pier there were four three pounder stone mortars with 262 balls.

There were also 49 muskets (of which 33 were out of order); 19 pistols (4 out of order); 83 pikes. The ammunition consisted of 213 musket rounds and 21,171 cartridges.

The complement of the island consisted of the Governor, two priests, one Treasury Official, three Officers, one surgeon, fifty soldiers, forty three convicts, one mason and one baker, totalling 103 persons.

Life in the Malvinas was hard and monotonous. The winter climate was cold, damp and windy. The houses were not very comfortable and military rountine was observed, with artillery and musket drills, cleaning and checking weapons, ship repairs, etc. Mass was held in the Chapel and some of the men herded cattle; amusements were few and consisted of card games and the occasional hunting expedition. Guards were mounted in Anunciacion Bay to warn of the arrival of unexpected ships or to report on anything unusual.

Without any doubt, one of the most important activities which were carried out, was the exploration and inspection tours of the Islands, the purpose of which was to prevent British sailors and fishermen from settling anywhere there.

The 30th of September 1781, Jacinto Altolaguirre reported that a reconnaissance of Port Egmont was made by Master Gunner José Morel.

In the month of April 1782 the ships transporting reliefs and stores arrived at the Malvinas; some officers and the two priest were changed and now the complement was 123 men.

Altolaguirre ordered Sublieutenant Vicente Villa to make another reconnaissance of Port Egmont, which he finished without incident in May 1782.

The first of April 1873, Commander Don Fulgencio Montemayor replaced Altolaguirre. Our young "criollo" officer pursued his career but unfortunately he fell sick and died in Madrid on the 26th August of 1787, with the rank of Lieutenant.

Thus the first "criollo" Governor of the Malvinas followed the destiny of sailors and died far from his native city and from his family.

The role which fate led him to play. helped him to sustain, through Spanish jurisdiction, the rights which his future independent and sovereign country were to inherit.

established settlements in Patagonia, or Puerto de la Cruzada (Port Egmont), or the Isla de los Estados, or in the Magellan Straits or in Cape Horn. The intention was to complete the surveys which Commander Clairac had been unable to finish.

The corvettes set sail for the Malvinas on the 13th of December to make an astronomical fix of the position of Puerto de la Cruzada (Port Egmont), while the brig "Nuestra Señora del Carmen" continued southwards on to San Julián, Rio Santa Cruz and Gallegos. On this voyage they encountered seven English and two French whaling ships and afterwards they returned to Montevideo.

As for Malaspina's corvettes, the "Descubierta" and the "Atrevida", they continued their voyage to the extreme west of the Malvinas, seeing on route a large number of whales, seals and water birds, which made Malaspina consider the importance of the future commercial development of this resource.

Lamentably, all this rich fauna for years suffered severe depradation by the English, the North Americans and the French.

Exploratory jorneys, maps and studies mark the passage of time and of famous corvettes, aboard one of which Lieutenant (junior grade) Francisco Xavier de Viana was travelling. He had been born in Montevideo. On the 20th of May 1790, Lieutenant Juan José de Elizalde reached the Malvinas on board the corvette "San Pio" and soon the hand-over took place.

That year an international event happened which had its repercussions in all the Spanish domains and also in the Malvinas Islands. Namely, the Nootka Sound Treaty of Agreement, signed between England and Spain.

Two British ships were stopped at Nootka Sound, in Vancouver, Canada, for having entered waters under Spanish jurisdiction. This information reached the Spanish Court at the end of 1789 and as had happened in the case of the Malvinas, the British considered that their honour had been sullied and they demanded satisfaction plus the return of the ships.

William Pitt "the Younger" was British Prime Minister at the time, and he started preparations for going to war. Spain did likewise. It was not possible for the Spanish Royal Navy to take on the British squadron alone, because the latter was larger. Therefore Spain appealed to France, then under Louis XVI, but really ruled by the National Assembly, one of whose most important members was Mirabeau. France once more proved to be reticent with her ally and the English and the Spanish started negotiations, through which the former obtained a great many advantages.

On the 28th of October 1790 at Saint Lawrence, the Nootka Sound Convention was signed, through which Spain, in spite of the efforts put forward by Floridablanca, conceded many points, in the light of the unfavourable military position she found herself in, due to the defection of her ally. England was to receive back what had been taken away from her at Nootka; she was to receive reparations for the damages incurred, and subjects of either power should not be stopped when fishing or sailing in the Pacific Ocean or in the *southern seas,* when landing on the coasts surrounding, these seas, in unoccupied stretches, when trading with the inhabitants of the country, or when establishing settlements. Everything could be done, within the limitations set out by the following clauses:

The English had obtained everything they wanted: to trade with the Pacific, sail in the southern seas and fish or hunt more than ten leagues from the coast occupied by Spain. The only prohibition was to place English garrisons in deserted areas of the South, even though they were permitted to set up temporary facilities for whale and seal hunting.

The fact that articles six and seven forbade the placement of settlements on the eastern and western coasts of the southern seas as well as in the already occupied adjacent islands, was a recognition of sovereignty over Carmen de Patagones, San José, Deseado and Port Soledad in the Malvinas.

The Nootka Sound treaty or agreement even though disadvantageous for Spain, represented British recognition of Spanish sovereignty

Article four established that British maritime activities should not serve "as a pretext for an illicit trade with Spanish settlements" and with this in mind it was specifically stipulated that "British subjects cannot sail nor fish in said seas within a distance of ten maritime leagues of any coastline already occupied by the Spaniards".

Article five referred to the freedom of being able to trade with the northeastern part of North America, to the north of the area already occupied by the Spaniards, and where neither of the two maritime powers had established settlements, either could trade without any impediments.

Article six stipulated that both in the eastern as well as in the western coasts of South America and the adjacent islands, in the future the respective subjects could not establish any settlements in those parts of the coast located to the south of the parts of the coasts and the adjacent islands already occupied by Spain. But the respective subjects would retain the right to land on the coasts and islands located there, so as to fish and so as to erect temporary dwellings and other buildings serving only towards this purpose.

Article seven pointed out that if any of the above clauses were to be infringed, the officers of both Parties, without undertaking any military action themselves, had to submit a precise report of the events to their respective Courts.

over the Malvinas. Spain had been occupying these islands by herself for 16 years, after England abandoned them in 1774.

It is true that no one knew for how long England would respect this agreement taking into account its aggressive policy, but this was a legal document which nullified alleged English rights claimed in later days.

Lieutenant Juan José de Elizalde was governor of the Malvinas from the middle of 1790 until May 1791.

The Royal Maritime Fishing Company had been formed in Madrid on November 1789, then in 1790 it started operations in Deseado and towards 1791 in Maldonado and Gorriti island.

Company production was unsatisfactory because of lack of opportunities and too much bureaucracy, but somehow the presence of the Royal Company and its ships represented the presence of Spain in our southern seas. As we have seen, the company planned to extend its operations to the Malvinas. This is the reason for the order to support the governors of the islands.

Lieutenant Pedro Pablo Sanguinetto replaced Elizalde and was governor during three terms.

In the inventory of batteries and buildings, Sanguinetto reported: 1) the "San Carlos" battery had two six-pound guns and four three-pound guns and four empty emplacements; 2) the "Santiago" had four twenty-four-pound guns in good condition; 3) the "San Felipe" had two eight-pound guns and an empty emplacement.

There were 38 buildings, 14 made of stone, as well as the pier and the bridge.

The brick kiln was useless, as well as two or three "green sod" houses which were in poor condition while several others were in need of repair.

Cattle registered a tremendous increase during that year, totaling 3,460 head, and this might have been due to a better head count.

The main concern of the governors of the Malvinas was the presence of foreign seal and whale hunters, particularly English and Americans. In a report to Mr. Antonio Valdes dated August 1, 1792, Sanguinetto noted that to that date an American sloop, and an English frigate and a schooner had entered Puerto Soledad using as an excuse to do so their need to repair damages.

Meanwhile Sanguinetto's replacement, Lieutenant Juan Jose de Elizalde had to carry out a reconnaissance mission in the South of Argentina before taking over the governorship of the Malvinas. He had to make a topographical survey of the eastern coast of Tierra del Fuego, which was practically unknown with the exception of what had been surveyed by the expedition of the Nodal brothers. He was also supposed to explore the area to locate the alleged English settlement "New Ireland" either in Magallanes, Tierra del Fuego or on the Isla de los Estados.

The corvette "San Pio" and the brigantine "Nuestra Señora del

Carmen", under the command of the experienced pilot Jose de la Peña set sail on December 20, 1791. They carried out one of the southernmost explorations of Tierra del Fuego, arrived at the southern coast of Isla Grande, sighted Isla Nueva and it was mere chance thay they did not discover the Beagle Channel. Warrant Officer Candido de Lasala, from Buenos Aires, joined that voyage as soldier of fortune.

After their discoveries they turned towards the Malvinas and arrived in Port Soledad on February 21, 1792, when Elizalde took over the governorship.

Since a war with France was expected in 1793, the Governor of the Malvinas prepared his colony and its 183 men for battle.

Candido de Lasala was one of Elizalde's seconds in the command of the "San Carlos" battery. Sanguinetto, with the rank of commander, took over the government of the islands in 1793 and then again in 1795.

The islands were not only a governorship but also a naval command.

As regards Warrant Officer Candido de Lasala, he had already requested his transfer to the Spanish Royal Navy in 1792. And it was thanks to the Viceroy and his commander, Juan Jose de Elizalde, who commended his "excellent conditions to serve in the navy" that he was authorized to do so on July 31, 1792, returning to the corvette "San Pio" with the rank of Lieutenant J.G.

Lasala belonged to a French noble family and two of his brothers had already joined the Royal Navy. To become an officer in the Spanish Royal Navy it was required that the four branches of grandparents be of noble ascent.

After his return he was posted to Europe, where he served on different ships and on land, returning to the Rio de la Plata ten years later on the frigate "Astrea", in 1803. Glory and death were waiting for him in his native country.

The clergymen who had been Franciscans and members of the order of la Merced were replaced as of 1793 by lay chaplains to accompany the navy chaplains who performed their duties on board the different ships.

Several expeditions against seal hunters were carried out, but the hunters were treated moderately well because England was considered a potential ally of Spain against France.

In 1799 a new governor of Malvinas took office. He deserves a closer look due to the fact that he had been born in the Banda Oriental (later Uruguay) and was the second creole governor of the islands.

Francisco Xavier de Viana was born in Montevideo on December 3, 1764, and he was the son of Jose Joaquin de Viana, Field-marshal and a former governor of Montevideo. His mother was Francisca de Alzaibar. His parents were both Spanish.

Viana joined the Royal Company of Cartagena as midshipman on December 10, 1778. He sailed in different ships and took part in the attacks on Gibraltar.

A fact that showed how capable the young second lieutenant was is that he was selected by the already famous Commander Alejandro Malaspina to crew his frigate "Astrea" on which he went around the world, in the service of the Royal Company of the Philippines. At the end of this trip, Viana was promoted to lieutenant.

The voyage of the "Astrea" was the forerunner of Malaspina's important scientific expedition which he undertook with the corvettes "Descubierta" and "Atrevida".

In this very long trip Francisco Xavier de Viana and his colleagues did a tremendous job. They surveyed the Rio de la Plata in 55 days and visited the officers of the Naval Station, one of whom was Commander Santiago de Liniers.

While his colleagues drew up the map, Viana was left in charge of the corvette "Descubierta", making it ready to continue its voyage. His work deserved the approval of Malaspina.

He was promoted twice during the expedition thanks to the favorable word put in by Malaspina; once in 1789 to Lieutenant (J.G.), and in 1793 to Lieutenant. This officer was so devoted to his duty that during this trip he was called from Montevideo to take care of some inheritance matters and instead of asking for leave he requested that the matter be postponed until his return.

While carrying out other missions and exploring the Brazilian coast the young naval officer from the Rio de la Plata was posted to the Malvinas with the corvette "Descubierta" in his command. This was the same corvette that had participated in the Malaspina expedition. The "Atrevida" also made trips to and was stationed in Malvinas at times.

The old "green sod" chapel, every year more dilapidated, continued to be used while the building of the new one continued very slowly. As we have seen the new one was started by Second Lieutenant Aldana in 1749.

Mr. Andres Acuña, a surgeon, Second Pilot Francisco Mas y Canella and staff Midshipman Jose Pereyra also travelled on the "Descubierta".

The crew included 11 navy officers, 28 marines and 6 gunners; 22 navy artillerymen, 18 sailors and 30 cabin boys and one page, which made a total of 127 people.

We give more detailed figures for some years because we think they give a clear idea about the population of the colony.

Life had few attractions there, being work to be done, hunting when the weather was good and attendance at mass. Occasionally there were some makeshift theater performances of religious or ethical plays. Troops were kept busy with guard duty and artillery drills while the sailors sewed sails, repaired the rigging and the hulls of their ships, when they were not sailing around the islands.

By 1798 cattle had decreased to 1,567 head, evidence that many were slaughtered to feed the people who lived on the islands.

Francisco Xavier de Viana arrived to take over as governor in May of 1800.

He reported that the houses and buildings in the Malvinas were dilapidated along with other deficiencies.

Viana alao sent a report on the condition of the bay and buildings in Port Soledad on February 28, 1801.

These are the links through which Argentine blood, closely interwoven with political events, forms one solid block of history, which spans the Spanish period and the period of independent sovereignty.

Fulgencio Montemayor took over the Islands without knowing that in Spain he had been promoted to the rank of Captain and he only found this out on his return from the Islands, when he finished his term of office on the 28th of June 1784. He had been sent to the Malvinas because Spain was at war with England.

Montemayor was succeeded by officers of lesser rank. By Lieutenant Don Agustin Figueroa until mid-1785, who in turn was succeeded by Commander Don Ramon Clairac y Villalonga. The latter was Governor of the Islands for three periods. He pursued sealers and whalers, he explored the coasts of Patagonia, he carried out the annual inspection tour of Port Egmont. Clairac was sworn in as Governor in 1785, 1787 and 1789 respectively. He took turns with Lieutenant Mesa y Castro and during his terms of office, buildings which were in ruins were repaired and extensive lengthy expeditions were undertaken, the purpose of which was to ensure the safety of the Islands and of the coasts of Patagonia. He also charted the Malvinas.

In 1778 there were 2,180 head of beef cattle and 166 mares. Many English and American sealers and whalers were marauding around the Islands. They were stopped and were inspected by the Spanish ships which prohibited hunting, but in practice this activity was difficult to detect.

The hard and quiet life in Puerto Soledad was to be shaken up by a piece of news which was to bring about a ceremony with the greatest show possible considering the scarcity of means available. King Carlos III of Spain had died on the 14th of December of 1788 and his son Carlos IV ascended the throne. The news arrived in the Malvinas more than ten months later.

Governor Clairac himself reported in full detail on the ceremonies and celebrations which had taken place: "A large stage was built with four angled corners supported by twenty arches with their respective staircases and handrails and on this stage a platform was placed with the portrait of His Majesty. Eight cypresses were placed around it in strategic postions serving as flagpoles for the respective flags of Spain. The Royal Standard was placed in the main arch, in the middle.

The swearing of allegiance to the New Monarch was carried out on the 4th of November 1789. Don José Blas Parexa, the Treasury Official, acted as the Royal Representative. The Royal Standard was borne to the Church in an official solemn procession led by the Governor, his officers and all the troops of the garrison on horseback. In the beautifully decorated and illuminated Chapel the Tedeum was sung.

An improvised bull-ring was built with terraced seats and a balcony. For the bull-fight eight individuals (we do not know whether they were volunteers or not) dressed up for the respective roles (matador, etc.). Twelve bulls were fought, four per afternoon, in three days of bull-fights.

Also, in the Navy barracks, comedies were performed on an improvised stage. For three nights the main buildings of the township were specially lit up.

A battery of twenty guns was brought ashore from the "Santa Elena" and lined up between the Hospital and the Chapel. There were bonfires and fireworks, all this so as to simulate a naval battle between two three-deck ships, which were specially built for the occasion, with a length of 3.75 metres each. On the last night of the celebrations, these mock-ups were burnt.

There is no doubt that these celebrations helped to break the monotony of the island life and the meat from the twelve bulls sacrificed in the bull-fights must have been well received.

At the end of 1789, the first two corvettes of an expedition led by the then Captain Don Alejandro Malaspina, arrived at the Malvinas Islands.

This formidable scientific, political and artistic expedition carried on board the best crews of the Royal Spanish Navy, as well as a group of naturalists, cartographers and artists difficult to surpass.

The expedition had sailed from Cadiz on the 30th of July 1789 and arrived at the Rio de la Plata on the 20th of September 1789.

The Viceroy entrusted the brig "Nuestra Señora del Carmen" to the expert pilot Don José de la Peña y Zurueta, so that he escort the corvettes along the Patagonian coast. He was the best choice because of his experience in our southern waters, his great nautical talents and his knowledge, of our coasts, and of of the coastlines of the Malvinas. Also, he was a good friend of the Indians who inhabited our Southern latitudes.

The expedition arrived at Deseado on the 2nd of December, after having sighted an English sealer, and there met up with de la Peña y Zurueta's brig.

The Viceroy also entrusted Malaspina with the mission of inspecting the coastline to make sure that the English had not meanwhile

The battery called "San Marcos" (previously "San Carlos") had its guns in "Santiago's" where all the guns had been placed. It did not have a moat and the embankment was in good condition. The "San Felipe" battery did not have any guns and the emplacement was useless.

As regards the buildings, there were 26 in all, 12 made of stone and the rest of "green sod". The old church was completely useless, and although the walls had been repaired and the roof fixed it was in bad condition. The other buildings were in good condition, which is proof of the activity carried out by this governor who managed to have all the buildings in good shape.

Due to his bad health Viana was relieved of duty. Upon arrival in Montevideo he requested transfer to the Army. He was appointed Sargeant Major and held different positions; he gave an outstanding performance in the defense of Montevideo during the English invasion of 1807.

In 1811 Francisco Xavier de Viana y Alzaibar joined the May revolution where he participated prominently. In 1813 he was appointed Governor Administrator in Cordoba and in 1814 the Director Posadas appointed him Secretary of War and Navy, rising to the rank of Brigadier General.

During the government of Alvear, Viana continued as Secretary of War and Navy, but when Alvear was ousted he fell from grace and was sent to prision, and later was released for health reasons. He went to Montevideo where he died in 1820.

Commander Bernardo Bonavía was governor of the Malvinas at three different times, from 1802 until 1803; from 1804 until 1805 and from 1806 until 1808. During this last period and as a result of the English invasions he did not receive supplies and went through difficult times.

Bonavía joined the May Revolution and rendered valuable services to the cause. He was an elderly man, who was born in Castilla in 1745, so during his last term as governor he was 63 years old.

The last governors of the Malvinas were Gerardo Bordas and Pablo Guillen. The first one was a merchant pilot and after finishing his term he was promoted to Lieutenant (J.G.) of the Royal Navy.

Pablo Guillen, second pilot of the Royal Navy arrived in the islands on January 8, 1810, and together with Bordas, outgoing governor, swore allegiance to Fernando VII with the usual ceremonies.

Once the May Revolution took place, a junta met in Montevideo and decided to regroup forces and evacuate the far away population of Malvinas. For this purpose the brigantine "Galvez" was sent to the south, under the command of pilot Manuel Moreno.

Pablo Guillen complied with the orders received to evacuate 46 men of the garrison, load the guns, weapons, file papers, etc.

A very important deed was that a lead plaque was nailed to the belfry of the Royal Chapel of the Malvinas with the following inscription:

"This island together with its Ports, Buildings, Outbuildings and everything in them belongs to Fernando VII, King of Spain and the Indies, Soledad de Malvinas, February 7th, 1811, being governor Pablo Guillen".

The same inscription was placed on the doors of the thirty odd buildings. A memorandum was prepared making reference to all this and was duly signed by Governor Guillen, Manuel Moreno and the Vicar of the islands, Juan Canosa, dated February 13, 1811 in the Colony of Soledad de Malvinas.

That same day or the following one the ships set sail and abandoned the Malvinas with the idea of returning there.

All this was inherited by Argentina.

From 1767 until 1811 the Malvinas were Spanish and during these years there were an uninterrupted series of governors. In 1811 the islands were evacuated but without giving them up. As we can see, the islands had never been British.

Our sovereign right to the islands is based on the historical possession of the Malvinas by the Spaniards, with 20 governors, who ruled the islands without interruption during 31 terms, and on the fact that Spain maintained a penintentiary, a colony and a port there for 43 years.

CHAPTER VI

The presence of Argentina in the Malvinas (1811—1833)

Our country inherited from Spain the rights to its territory, of which the Malvinas are a part.

From 1811 until 1820 the islands were not occupied; then on November 6, 1820, the Argentine flag was hoisted and three Argentine military commanders ruled the islands until 1824, in the meantime the government gave concessions to Angel Pacheco and, in 1829, Vernet was appointed first Political and Military governor of the Malvinas.

After an attack by the American frigate "Lexington", another governor was appointed, Major Mestivier, who was murdered by his men.

Navy Lieutenant Colonel Jose Maria Pinedo with the schooner "Sarandi" remained in charge of the islands. Finally, on January 3, 1833, an English attack ended our occupation of the islands.

This summary of events show that as heirs or true occupants of the islands, we exercised our sovereignty uninterruptedly and we only abandoned the islands when force was used against us.

When the Spaniards evacuated Malvinas, leaving intact the rights Fernando VII, Argentines had already started their of independence movement.

An administrative occurrence made the Revolutionary Junta aware very soon of the existence of a problem which had to be solved in connection with the Malvinas, since it was under its jurisdiction.

Doctor Ernesto J. Fitte, found an administrative procedure started by Mr. Gerardo Bordas upon his return from serving as governor in the Malvinas requesting payment of his salary and gratuities, which were equivalent to that received while serving in a warship at sea.

The Head of the Naval Station in Montevideo did not have instructions from the Viceroy regarding Borda's request to be paid gratuities equivalent to those of a commander of a warship, so he turned over the request to Viceroy Cisneros on March 9, 1810, for him to decide as to whether the officers of the Royal Treasury had to meet this payment or not. Viceroy Cisneros answered on March 20th, but the answer was delayed due to bureaucratic procedures, so that Zalazar from Montevideo had to repeat his request on May 20th, but this time the new Junta presided by Cornelio Saavedra had to answer the request. It did so in a letter signed by the President of the Revolutionary Junta and the Secretary, Juan Jose Paso, in the following terms:

French Bay, according to Pellion (1820). View of the "L'Uranie" encampment in Frech Bay in the Malvinas Islands.

"In a communication dated December 13th, I told Your Excellency the following:

"Today I am sending to the Navy Commander of this Naval Station the following letter: Having observed that the High Board of the Royal Treasury in charge of apportioning all expenditures and payments has approved that the Malvinas settlement be given the same treatment as that given to a ship at sea and that all men be considered as part of the crew of the ship. . . henceforth all salaries, gratuities, wages and other expenses incurred in said settlement or pertaining to it, whatever type they may be, shall be paid by the Navy commander of this Naval Station. . ." and went on to say that it was passing this information to the corresponding officers of the Royal Treasury and to the Lieutenant General of the Army finally ordering that a copy of the resolution be sent to "the Commander of the Navy".

It ended with the words "God Keep Your Excellency for many years. Buenos Aires, May 30, 1810. Cornelio Saavedra, Juan José Paso. Secretary. To the Ministers of the Royal Treasury".

Thus the first Argentine government continued exerting sovereignty over the islands.

The war of independence and the problems derived from internal struggles prevented an effective occupation of the islands, which were left without authorities until the end of 1820.

During this long period of time the only visitors to the islands were whale and seal hunters, who visited the coasts to hunt, replenish the ships' drinking water supply or slaughter cattle which roamed on the islands.

During the Spanish domination there were up to 5,000 head of cattle but by 1804 there were only 235 head, and 739 horses. This means that several dozen head of cattle and horses were left in Malvinas by the Spaniards and cattle multiplied in freedom, although many were slaughtered by seal hunters.

After May 1810, the different governments which followed were beset by very serious problems: the war of independence, the search for a political path to follow and the type of government to use, the fighting between Buenos Aires and the provinces of the interior. It was a struggle for survival and only after San Martin's campaigns removed the danger of a Spanish restoration, and when Riego's revolution put an end to the last large expedition to America, only then it was possible to look at the territory as a whole and to think about the Malvinas.

This does not mean that all the problems had been completely solved, because once the Spanish threat had decreased, anarchy was rampant in the country and it was in 1820 that Belgrano died in total despair caused by the military, political and moral defeats suffered. It was precisely Belgrano who wrote a story describing the Malvinas in the

Frigate Heroína in Puerto Soledad, flying the flag. Malvinas Islands, 6th November 1820.

paper "Correo de Comercio" the first one to draw attention to them.

The Argentine flag was hoisted in the Malvinas by the frigate "Heroina", under the command of Colonel David Jewett and it represented an act of sovereignty over the islands which at the time was accepted by the different nations of the world, since nobody protested nor made any claims.

David Jewett was born in North Parish, New London, Connecticut, on June 17, 1772. He studied law, joined the American Navy and was the commanding officer of a vessel called "Trumball" with which he obtained a considerable booty. In 1801, as a result of a military reform, he lost his post in the Navy but then in 1812, as a result of the war of his country against England, he participated as a privateer.

David Jewett offered his services to the Argentine authorities to help them in their fight for independence and carried out some praiseworthy campaings as privateer.

In 1820 he was appointed Commander of the pirate frigate "Heroina", with which he made an ill-fated campaign where he faced mutiny and scurvy. Finally, the privateer commander headed for the Malvinas to hoist the Argentine flag there, following instructions from the government. By then the "Heroina" was considered a "state vessel" that is to say a regular ship and not a pirate one.

At the end of October, and with a reduced crew due to casualties suffered from scurvy, the frigate entered Bahia Anunciacion in Soledad island and cast anchor in front of the ruins of the former Spanish capital.

In the vicinity there were fifty seal hunters with their ships.

On November 6, 1820, Navy Colonel David Jewett, commander of the frigate "Heroina", hoisted the blue and white flag in the ruins of Port Soledad (former Port Louis).

The occupation of the islands was done with all formalities and it was preceded by a notice from Jewett to the English and American seal hunters and fishermen who used the islands at will. The notice read as follows: "State frigate Heroina, in Port Soledad, November 2, 1820. Sir, I have the honour of informing you that I have arrived in this port with a commission from the Supreme Government of the United Provinces of the Rio de la Plata to take possession of the islands on behalf of the country to which they belong by Natural Law. While carrying out this mission I want to do so with all the courtesy and respect for all friendly nations; one of the objectives of my mission is to prevent the destruction of resources necessary for all ships passing by and forced to cast anchor here, as well as to help them to obtain the necessary supplies, with minimum expenses and inconvenience. Since your presence here is not in competition with these purposes and in the belief that a personal meeting will be fruitful for both of us, I invite you to come aboard, where you'll be welcomed to stay for as long as you wish; I would also

David Jewett. Marine Colonel of Provincias Unidas de Sud America And Commander of the Frigate "Heroína".

greatly appreciate your extending this invitation to any other British subject found in the vicinity; I am, respectfully yours". Signed, Jewett, Colonel of the Navy of the United Provinces of South America and commander of the frigate "Heroina". (We should not be surprised by this reference to South America, because the idea was to liberate all of South America).

When Jewett was released of his command, Guillermo Mason took over the "Heroina" and for a few days he ruled the islands, thus becoming the second military commander there.

Even though the Argentine flag had been hoisted in the islands, the departure of the "Heroina" and subsequent lack of authorities enabled the English, North Americans and some creole hunters to loot the islands without any restriction.

Jewett's formal possession of the islands on behalf of the Government of Buenos Aires became known abroad and a story was published by the "Redactor" of Cadiz, in August, 1821, from reports heard in Gibraltar. Also the "Gaceta de Salem" ("Salem's Gazette) reported it in the middle of 1821. Thus, everybody was aware of this fact either by the stories published or by accounts of the seal hunters who witnessed the ceremony.

Neither at this time nor for many years to come did England protest or claim its alleged rights to the islands.

In order to exert its sovereignty over the islands the government took some measures which were promptly executed. At this time two important figures of our history appear: Jorge Pacheco and Luis Vernet.

Jorge Pacheco was born in Buenos Aires on April 25, 1761, and started his military career with the rank of second lieutenant of the Lancers in Buenos Aires. The lancers were in charge of protecting the frontier line against the Indians and Pacheco suffered all the hardships of this type of life, since he belonged to a small, ill equipped group of the army with the duty of protecting civilization from Indian attacks.

By January 8, 1799, Jorge Pacheco was already captain of the Lancers in Montevideo and took part in three campaigns against the Charrua Indians. In 1810, he gave his whole-hearted support to the May Revolution and became captain of the militia.

Luis Vernet was born in Hamburg on March 6, 1791, of French ancestors. When he was 14 years old his father sent him to the United States where he worked for a German business company. He did very well due to his natural intelligence and skill in business.

After travelling through Europe he came to Buenos Aires in 1817, where he carried out different business activities with varying degrees of success. This prompted him to become a broker, an activity which enabled him to make use of his European connections.

On August 17, 1819, Luis Vernet married Maria Saez in Buenos Aires. She had been born in the Banda Oriental (later Uruguay) and was the daughter of Colonel Francisco Saez and Josefa Perez, both natives also of the Banda Oriental. The ceremony was performed according to the Roman Catholic rite as recorded in the files of the Church of la Merced.

After the departure of the "Heroina" from the Malvinas the government of Buenos Aires continued to excercise its sovereignty over the islands for some years.

On August 23, 1823, Jorge Pacheco was granted a concession to slaughter cattle and seals in Soledad island. Pacheco's partner was Luis Vernet.

In 1824, Pacheco and Vernet attempted to make a settlement on the islands but failed. Between January and April of that same year the government appointed Pablo Areguati —a captain in the Entre Rios militia, who had been appointed major of Mandisovi in 1811 by Belgrano— to become the third military commander of the Malvinas.

Vernet who had an energetic personality, undertook the settlement of the islands, shipped horses and sheep to the Malvinas and had some dilapidated buildings in Port Soledad repaired.

On January 5, 1828, the government through a decree signed by Dorrego and Balcarce, improved the terms of the concessions made to Pacheco, with the understanding that Vernet would be the guiding force in this endeavour.

Vernet did an excellent job in the settlement of the islands, simultaneously carrying out scientific work in order to provide a better knowledge of the islands.

Vernet's studies and reports included information about the Indians, possible location of other settlements, sources of income, etc. He was a pioneer interested in the exploitation of Patagonia, particularly of the Isla de los Estados. Unfortunately, Argentines and their government were too busy fighting each other in civil wars.

The Argentine government, represented by Buenos Aires, was in charge of Patagonian and Malvinas affairs as it had been the case before independence and thought something should be done to recognize Vernet's work in the promotion of new commercial areas and in conforming Argentina's sovereignty over the area. Accordingly, Vernet was appointed First Political and Military Governor of the Malvinas. We already know that Jewett and Mason had been de facto Military Commanders of the islands. Vernet was the fourth Argentine officer to be appointed to the Malvinas, but with a broader title which encompassed both civilian and military attributions.

The following historical decree was issued on June 10, 1829:

"When as a result of the glorious revolution of May 25, 1810, these provinces became independent from the Mother Country, Spain, had effective possession of the Malvinas and all the other islands which surround Cape Horn, even the one which is known as Tierra del Fuego. This possession was justified by the right of first occupation, by the consent given by the main European maritime powers and by the proximity of these islands to the Continent part of the Viceroyalty of Buenos Aires, entitled to govern them. For these reasons, and since the Government of the Republic has inherited all the rights the old Mother Country had over these Provinces, and which were exercised by the viceroys, it has continued to exert its authority on said islands, their ports and coastal areas. And even though it has not been possible to give to that part of the territory of the Republic the attention and care deserved, it is no longer possible to delay the adoption of measures to ensure the rights of the Republic enabling it to benefit from the production of said islands and to give the population the protection it deserves; the Government agrees and decrees:

"Article 1: The Malvinas and other islands adjacent to Cape Horn in the Atlantic Ocean will be ruled by the Political and Military Commander, to be immediately appointed by the Government of the Republic."

"Article 2: The Political and Military Commander will live in Soledad island, where a battery will be set up, under the flag of the Republic."

"Article 3: The Political and Military Commander will enforce the laws of the Republic on said islands as well as the regulations regarding fishing and seal hunting along its coasts."

"Article 4: Let this decree be known".

"Signed: Martin Rodriguez. Salvador M. del Carril."

The reasons invoked in this decree cannot be more clear, concise and true to history. The Argentine Republic had no doubts about its sovereign rights not only over the Malvinas, but also over the islands in the neighborhood of Cape Horn, that is to say over Isla de los Estados, Nueva, Picton, Lennox and other archipelagos close to the bleak southern cape.

On that same day Luis Vernet was appointed by the Government First Political and Military Governor of the islands under the following terms:

"The Government of Buenos Aires having decreed on this day that the Malvinas Islands adjacent to Cape Horn in the Atlantic sea be ruled by a political and military commander and keeping in mind the capabilities of Luis Vernet, has decided to appoint him, as it is being done by means of this document, for said position as Political and Military Commander of the Malvinas, bestowing onto him all the authority and jurisdiction necessary to fulfill his job. Signed: Martin Rodriguez, Salvador M. del Carril." Stamp.

Vernet also received a signed and stamped diploma. Vernet had

Luis Vernet. First Political and Military Governor of the Malvinas Islands (1829 - 1833).

told the government many times that it was necessary to build a for on the islands and had requested that he be given guns to fortify it. He also thought that a warship was necessary "to cruise those seas to enforce the Law for Fishing Protection" and that it was convenient to have a small ship with a gun to collect fishing duties, haul wood to the strait of Magellan and have permanent communication with Rio Negro and Buenos Aires. Vernet had other requests too but was opposed to the construction of a penitentiary, because he thought this would drive away future settlers and settling companies.

The government ordered that Vernet be given four eight pound guns and their ammunition, 50 rifles with ammunition and belting, 2,000 pounds of iron, bellows and other forging instruments to set up a blacksmith shop in Soledad island.

Meanwhile, what was England's attitude while all this was going on, taking into account that it was a proclamation of Argentina's sovereignty?

Ever since Jewett hoisted our flag in the islands, on November 6, 1820, she had kept silent. Likewise in 1825 when the Treaty of Friendship, Trade and Navigation was signed between both nations, but then on November 19, 1829, the English representative, Woodbine Parish, protested to our government for issuing the decree which created the Political and Military District of Malvinas.

On August 8, 1829, the Foreign Office had sent a letter to Parish complaining that the acts of possession on the part of the Buenos Aires government affected the rights of British sovereignty over the islands. These rights were becoming increasingly important because the islands were used to supply commercial ships and repair English warships in the "western hemisphere". Parish was not told whether the English government would take over the islands or whether this was appropriate or not, just that it should be treated as a "delicate issue" and related to important matters. When the English government learnt about the decree issued by the Argentine government, on June 10, 1829, Parish was ordered to present a formal complaint for the "advances made by our Government".

As Jose Arce points out very accurately, England was forgetting:

1) She had left the islands unattended since 1774 (for fifty five years).

2) She knew that Spain had occupied Port Soledad in East Malvina since Boungainville's departure in 1767.

3) She had accepted the declaration of Prince Masserano, Spanish Ambassador in 1771, recognizing "Spain's sovereignty over the Malvinas".

4) She had abandoned Port Egmont in 1774.

5) She was aware that the Government of Buenos Aires had inherited from Spain the rights over the islands after 1810, the year when the revolution for emancipation started.

6) She was aware of the declaration of independence of the United Provinces of the Rio de la Plata (1816).

7) She had recognized their independence and had signed with the United Provinces a friendship and trade treaty. (February 1825).

8) She did not ignore that since 1820 three military commanders and one governor had represented the Buenos Aires government in the Malvinas. We would like to add that in 1749 England had recognized Spain's sovereignty over the islands but not respected it during 1765/66 and that by the Nootka Sound Treaty, signed in 1790 she had recognized all of Spain's possessions, including the Malvinas.

The English position was very weak from a political and legal point of view but very strong from a military and naval stance.

After his appointment, the new governor travelled to the colony with 15 Englishmen and 23 Germans, including wives and children; in addition to servants, black and white, gauchos and indians.

On July 15th, Vernet's wife Maria Saez arrived in the Malvinas with her children Emilio, Luisa and Sofia. A fourth child was born on February 5, 1830, and she was named Malvina. His actions reflected his attitude towards his position, that of an Argentine official, and a respect for the land which had welcomed him.

Now let us go back to the new political and military governor of the Malvinas and we will see how he carried out his mission with much energy, progress and success.

The island became something like a factory and the capital was Port Soledad, which Vernet renamed Port Luis.

One of the main activities was the slaughter of wild cattle which roamed all over the island. The gauchos performed all the tasks connected with this activity. Another occupation was seal hunting, not only in the Malvinas but also in the Isla de los Estados, which was part of his territory.

The population of Port Luis varied in number, because even though some were permanent dwellers, others were fishermen, hunters, scientists and tradesmen which spent only part of their time there or stayed for short periods.

The permanent population was comprised of more than one hundred people. A. Gomez Langenheim says there were more than 120, including wives, single women and children. There were more people when merchant vessels, sealing ships or scientific boats arrived; then the population increased to two or three hundred people. We should recall that some ships were at the orders of or chartered by Vernet. These boats fished, hunted or sailed to the Isla de los Estados to load wood.

In the diaries left from those days, particularly in Vernet's and his wife's, as well as in the memoirs and documents written by Vernet, one can get a good idea of the active life they led. The settlers had to build and repair houses, storing sheds for supplies and seal skins, tools and also fish, hunt, salt fish, repair boats and also many other activities.

The production of the island was mainly cow hides, salted meat, tallow, seal skins and even rabbit skins; these were not only sent to Buenos Aires where they sold well but also exported to England, mainly seal and cow skins.

Wood and fish in brine also sold well.

The above is an indication of Vernet's progressive spirit and how the population prospered because they formed a hard-working colony.

We will transcribe a few paragraphs from Vernet's and his young wife's diary which were quoted by Langenheim, an author we've already mentioned. Vernet wrote the following:

"Sunday, May 25, 1828 — The weather is good although we had some squalls, with hail; there is a south west wind."

"We fired three gun shots at sunrise and at sunset.

"After eating meat and cakes which had been specially baked, we spent the afternoon shooting at a target and then after sunset people danced in the barrel maker's house until sunrise."

"Wednesday, July 9th. Cloudy and rainy with moderate south east winds.

Our people celebrated the formal declaration of Independence of Buenos Aires."

From the diary written in 1829 by Mrs. Maria Saez de Vernet, we quote the following:

"Sunday, August 2nd. It was cloudy and it drizzled all day long. The Captains had their meal with us and in the afternoon the negroes prepared their drums and the negro women dressed in their best clothes and donned the beads which I had brought them from Buenos Aires. Their dances are ugly, it is not possible to stand for very long the shouting which goes on all the time while they dance".

"Sunday, August 30th. It was a good day this festivity of Saint Rose of Lima, that is why Vernet decided today to take possession of the island on behalf of the Government of Buenos Aires. The inhabitants met at noon, the national flag was hoisted and a 21-gun salute was fired, continually repeating: Long live our country! I put in everybody's hat a ribbon with the two colours of our flag, and the Commander introduced himself".

These excerpts do not tell us about all the things that were done in the islands, but give us an idea of the authority, progress and intelligence on the part of the learned governor. It is worthwhile to

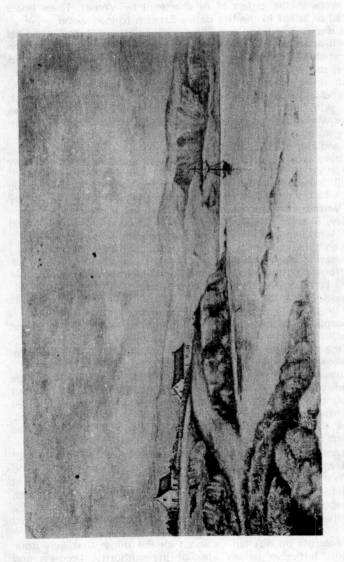

Malvinas Islands. View of Port Luis with the two main houses reconstructed by Luis Vernet on the Spanish ruins of Puerto Soledad (1829).

transcribe a translation of the opinions of Captain Fitz Roy, Vernet's guest: "He has a long and low house, it has only one floor and very thick walls made of stone. There I found a good library with Spanish, German and English books. We had an interesting conversation during our meal, with Mr. Vernet, his wife, Mr. Brisbane and others; that evening music was played and we danced. There was a big piano in the room, Mrs. Vernet, who is from Buenos Aires, sang in her excellent voice. All this seemed a bit odd in the Falklands where all we expected to find were seal hunters".

The colony did well and progressed, the settlers even though they had been worried in the beginning, had settled down and become accostumed to this rugged and peaceful life. Everything went on normally for the country and the governor until foreign intervention unleashed ruin and grief.

The cause which unleashed the events at the end of 1831 was the control over the plundering and destruction of the seal wealth existing in the islands.

The Governor of the Malvinas received continuous reports on the plundering carried out by seal hunters and had requested the government to send him a warship, even a small one with a single gun. It was practically impossible to arrest the many seal hunters which swarmed the ports and coves of the islands. However, Vernet decided to take some defensive action to protect his exclusive fishing rights, which were the rights of the nation delegated to him.

The seal hunters could not claim ignorance, because as soon as they approached the islands Vernet sent them a letter where he informed. . . "all Captains of the ships fishing in any part of the coast of my territory, I ask you to stop doing it, and if resistance is offered you"ll be seized by any warship belonging to the Republic of Buenos Aires, or by any of my boats, enforcing the authority which I have to apply the laws of the Republic. I also warn you against slaughtering cattle in the eastern island. . . etc. etc."

This notice was delivered to all ships arriving in the Malvinas. On one occasion Vernet discovered that three ships which had received repeated warnings, not only by means of the letter but had also been told that they would be seized if they continued coming back, kept on returning. The three sealing vessels were North American and had been around the islands for several months. So finally Vernet seized the three boats which were: "Brukwater", under captain Daniel Careu; "Harriet" under Captain Gilberto Davison and "Superior" under captain Esteban Congar.

After doing this, Vernet and his family departed for Buenos Aires to defend his case.

George W. Slacum, who had been Charge d'Affairs of the United States and who had replaced Mr. John Forbes as U.S. Consul in Buenos

Aires upon the latter's death, was not the most competent diplomat to carry out the negotiations. On the contrary he "totally lacked diplomatic experience as well as tact and good judgement", to quote the North American historian Julius Goebel, Jr.

Based on the statement by captain Davison, Slacum presented a complaint to the Government for the seizure of the "Harriet" on November 21, 1831. Buenos Aires' Foreign Minister, Tomas Manuel de Anchorena, answered that the matter was being considered by the Ministry of War and Navy. In a subsequent letter the U.S. Consul denied Vernet's right to seize North American seal hunters and fishermen in waters, coasts and archipelagos in the vicinity of Cape Horn. To make matters worse the commander of U.S. Navy corvette "Lexington", Silas Duncan, contacted Slacum because he had decided to "protect" the interest of the North American citizens involved in this affair.

Slacum' letters were answered by Anchorena who contended that since Slacum was only the consul he did not have the capacity nor the power to deal with this matter which pertained to both governments.

On December 9, 1831, the "Lexington" sailed to carry out its mission in the Malvinas and Anchorena informed Slacum in writing that if the commander of the "Lexington" damaged people or property in the Malvinas he would protest because the government of Argentina had to be respected.

Approximately at this time Slacum contacted Woodbine Parish and Mer Fox, British consul and representative who had asserted English claims on the Malvinas.

The U.S. corvette entered Bahia Anunciacion on December 27, 1831, at midnight, and the following day it anchored in front of Port Luis. But the North American corvette did not hoist its own flag, but the French one. Thus it was using a buccaneer tactic in a time of war!

The arrival was saluted from the port with the Argentine flag and then the powerful North American vessel commenced its "heroic task". The schooner "Aguila" was seized, as were two men, Brisbane and Mescalf, selected among the inhabitants of Port Luis. Then the North American flag was hoisted and the men landed, took over the buildings, spiked all the cannons, blew up all the ammunition and took whatever Captain Davison deemed belonged to him.

Davison's men destroyed storage sheds, knocked down doors, took 25 prisoners all of whom were released after being questioned with the exception of six who were considered to be the most important ones.

On January 21, 1832, the U.S. Navy corvette left the Malvinas and headed towards Montevideo leaving behind in ruins what had been until then a prosperous Argentine settlement. Mateo Brisbane and six other settlers were taken as prisoners and received very little food on board, while others who were considered passengers travelled in better conditions. An act of unheard abuse had taken place which probably represents one of the darkest events in the otherwise brilliant history of the United States navy.

Historian Julius Goebel, Jr., examined the binnacle of the "Lexington", but did not find any reference made by Silas Duncan about the events which took place at Port Luis. Probably he feared future problems because he knew he had not precisely accomplished a feat.

The "Lexington" arrived in Montevideo at the beginning of February and on the 10th the Argentine government was informed about the insult. Outrage was unanimous and the newspaper "Gaceta Mercantil" branded the action "a violation to international law" and "an insult to the Argentine flag".

Our Government severed its relations with Slacum because it considered him the principal author of this abuse.

Argentina has ever since been vigorously protesting to the United States and requesting indemnity; but its demands have not been met yet.

Had English and North American seal hunters any fishing and hunting rights in the Malvinas and our southern coast? In the northern hemisphere there were areas where fishing rights had been granted to other American or European nations more than a century ago, but we have seen that neither during the Spanish period nor after independence, fishing or hunting were permitted in the coasts of Malvinas, neighboring waters or along the coast all the way down to Cape Horn. Illegal fishing continued because it was impossible to control it. Thus, North American attitude had been unreasonable and against international law.

The "Redactor", a newspaper from New York, defended the Argentine position stating that the actions taken by the "Lexington" were against international law.

As we will see, Vernet was not reinstated as governor nor did he return to the islands. At the time he might have made some incorrect statements product of his bitterness and concern for the confusion which prevailed in the country. But we should not forget his talent. Not only while he was settling the islands but also later on when the Republic became united after Caseros. He protected its interests and made reports on the Malvinas. Later he carried out progressive and civilizing work in the area of San Isidro. His partner, Jorge Pacheco had died in 1832 and he died in 1871. He was an intelligent and capable man, who was very energetic and industrious and the country is indebted to him for his attempt to settle the Malvinas and his contribution to the development of southern Patagonia. It is sad he had to live in one of the worst periods of our history, during the civil wars.

Major Esteban Francisco Mestivier was appointed governor and he sailed with 25 men and a very young aide, Jose Antonio Gomila, on board the old flag ship of Admiral Brown, the schooner "Sarandí", which had been one of our most heroic ships in the war against Brazil.

The "Sarandi" arrived in the Malvinas with the new governor and nine days later, on November 24, 1832, it left to inspect the neighboring islands, including Tierra del Fuego and then return to the Malvinas. During this period Major Mestivier was dramatically murdered.

When Pinedo returned to the Malvinas he found a mutiny had taken place and he started the corresponding proceedings.

On January 2, 1833, the British corvette "Clio" arrived in Port Soledad. As it was customary Pinedo sent one of his officers to pay a courtesy visit to the British warship where he was informed that the Argentines should strike the colors and leave the island.

Pinedo reacted correctly. He faced a difficult situation, his ship was not as powerful as the English one, although he could put up a defense for some time. But he had other problems, too. The majority of his crew were Englishmen, with only a few Argentines. The second in command, Second Lieutenant Elliot was an American. He talked to all of them, the British said that they would carry out their duty, the pilot would do his job, but refused to fight. The five cabin boys, aged between 15 and 20 years old said they would fight, and the 80-men crew said they would do what they were told.

With this information Pinedo started to implement his plan, which was correct. He called in Gomila, who was under arrest, released him, gave him arms to distribute among the 18 soldiers of the garrison, and proceeded, to follow what he considered were the navy's instructions. Before leaving Buenos Aires he had received the navy code of honor, where article 9 says that whenever the Argentine flag be in danger due to the threat of an attack or occupation by a foreign power, the flag has to be defended until the very end. When Pinedo later on wrote his report about the events he began quoting the code. But as time went by Pinedo started to falter.

The British landed on January 3, 1833, at 9 a.m., first they hoisted their flag on a mast they had brought along, then they lowered our flag, folded it very carefully and sent in over to Pinedo. On January 5, Pinedo together with some of the local people on board sailed for Buenos Aires.

When the "Sarandi" arrived in Buenos Aires, Admiral Brown immediately offered his services to the government. The Argentines protested to London and while diplomatic exchanges took place, a report about what had happened was prepared, including the problems in the garrison, the murder, etc.

Sergeant Saenz Valiente, who had murdered Mestivier, was shot in the main square of Buenos Aires, after having his right hand amputated. Six other leaders who had participated in the murder were also shot with him. Pinedo, received a four month suspension from duty, a very light punishment indeed, and he was forced to leave the navy and posted to the army. (This should be explained: Pinedo in the army would have the rank of commander which did not make him eligible to have his own command whereas in the navy he could be the commander of a ship and he had proved already that he was uncapable of facing a dangerous situation.)

From then on, Argentina started to protest, the first claim made by Manuel Moreno, who received the answer that the British had never given up their sovereignty over the Malvinas.

Before Pinedo sailed from the Malvinas he appointed Political and Military Commander of the islands, a Frenchman named Juan Simon, who had been Vernet's trusted foreman in charge of his gauchos. But Simon's appointment was nominal because the royal authority was vested on J.J. Onslow of the British Royal Navy.

However, the "Clio" did not stay very long in the islands, sailing on January 14, 1833, without waiting for the "Tyne", a smaller ship, which arrived on January 16, and saluted the Union Jack. Before his departure, captain Onslow gave the job of hoisting the English flag on Sundays and on arrival of other ships to Guillermo Dickson, a Scot who was one of Vernet's trusted men.

The "Tyne" also sailed a few days later and the islands were left practically without any government. This situation prevailed during 1833. Something might have been done to recover the islands then if our countrymen had not been involved in permanent political and civil war.

The events of August 26, 1833, took place due to the absence of British authorities in the islands. On that day two gauchos and five Charrua Indians who worked the cattle in the fields, under orders of Antonio Rivero, arrived in Port Soledad and demanded Juan Simon they be given money instead of the vouchers they normally received. When Simon refused they cowardly murdered him as well as other men who had been loyal to Vernet; that is Brisbane, who was Vernet's trusted man, a German, a Spaniard and Dickson, a Scot who had been in charge of hoisting the English flag when English ships were sighted. After these murders, everybody was terrified and the remaining creole inhabitants of Soledad as well as the seal hunters of different nationalities that were around fled to a nearby islet, where they asked for help. An English ship came to their assistance and Navy Lieutenant Henry Smith, together with a non-commissioned officer and six marines landed and chased Rivero and his men, one of whom, Brasido, had already been killed. The seven men, including Rivero himself, surrendered one by one, Rivero being the last one.

Rivero and three other men were sent to England, but there the court ruled they could not be tried because the Malvinas had not been incorporated yet to the British Empire. So the men were returned to Montevideo where they were released.

This is the true story of what happened proof of which is stated in 42 documents published by the National Academy of History.

Attempts have been made to create a legend about courageous gauchos who attacked and defeated the British, but this is just imagination. The truth as recorded in those documents does not authorize the creation of myths or legends.

England recognized our independence in 1825 and signed a treaty of friendship, navigation and commerce; she was at peace and obtained large profits trading with our Nation. Even so she attacked a country she was friends with and usurped its Malvinas, taking advantage of its delicate domestic political situation.

All the Argentine population, the government and provincial governors alike, were all indignant at such a disgreceful usurpation and on the 17th of July 1833, the Argentine representative in London presented a paper of protest giving all the background information. In reply he was told that the Falklands were English. On the 29th of December 1833 he again insisted on the return of the Islands, but without results. In 1841 he repeated this once more and upon being rejected again said that "Buenos Aires will never be satisfied with the unfair English decision". The claim was cut short.

The country was reorganized in 1880 and four years later the Argentine Geographic Institute published a map which included the Malvinas. England protested and Minister Francisco J. Ortiz pointed out that the archipelago belonged to Argentina and not to England.

The claim continued in force, staunchly. Argentine sovereignty over the islands was not negotiated nor recognized.

CHAPTER VII

Almost a century and a half of British appropriation

British Royal Navy Lieutenant Henry Smith was the first English authority in the islands. It was a dubious military authority in an English dependency which did not have the category of a colony.

The history of the Malvinas from then on unfolded in accordance with English laws, life style and habits.

We have divided this period in three subperiods, on the basis of political, economic or legal events that took place in the Malvinas. We admit, however, that the limits between the subperiods are not very precise and are debatable.

The first subperiod covered the years from 1833 until 1866. It was during these years that England's appropriation became "legal" since it was performed during 1842. During this same year Port Luis was moved to Port Stanley and the mainstay of the islands was mainly wild cattle. Towards the end of this subperiod the number of cattle decreased and we witness the introduction of sheep. Seals were still hunted, either legally or illegally.

The second subperiod covered the years 1866—1908, when the colony was consolidated and under the rule of the Falkland Islands Company sheep became the main and most important source of income for the islands. This period ended with the increasing importance obtained by the Malvinas, as head of the "dependencies", which England took over in 1908.

The third subperiod started in 1908 and extends until to-day.

The population peak in the Malvinas was in 1911 due to the whaling industry.

The inhabitants of the Malvinas had a distinguished participation in the two world wars and this is a source of pride for the islanders. Actually we should consider separately the years between the end of second world war and today because of a new phase in Argentine-British diplomatic negotiations, of current situation in the islands in the light of the recent events, and of the progress registered there.

First Subperiod — Consolidation of British domination — 1833—1866

As we have already seen Lieutenant Henry Smith landed to restore order and to arrest Rivero and his men. Having done this he devoted his efforts to the reorganization of the colony which was in a dreadful condition.

There were around forty settlers including a few gauchos and the three courageous women who had endured so much suffering since the days when the colony was prosperous and belonged to Argentina.

Lieutenant Smith's son replaced Brisbane as administrator of Vernet's property. Meanwhile Vernet demanded that the English crown pay him £ 3,300 for the cattle which had been slaughtered and £ 14.296 as compensation for all his other properties, which included houses, horses, seal skins, domesticated cattle, etc. Lieutenant Smith wished to take care of this property but the Crown refused, pending a decision on whether it would recognize Vernet's property or compensate him for it. In the end no payment was made. Vernet continued putting in claims for several years and finally, twenty years later, poor and powerless he had to resign himself to its loss.

Meanwhile Lieutenant Smith was busy repairing houses and stockyards, tending wild cattle for the Crown and recording temperatures in Port Luis. Finally he resigned from his post during the summer of 1838 and Royal Navy Lieutenant Robert Locway was appointed to fill this position. This officer arrived from the Rio de la Plata on board the "Arrow" which was in the command of Lieutenant B.J. Sullivan, who had been commissioned to make a basic scientific survey of the islands. He was an experienced officer since he had been in the staff of the "Beagle". Locway took with him sheep, chickens and seeds.

According to Sullivan, Port Luis was very small at the time. It had two small houses, one of which was used as government house and three or four huts. There were 45 settlers, 25 men, 10 women and 10 children. Antonina Kinney, doctor-midwife of the village was one of the women listed; undoubtedly she is the Antonina Roxas who had taken part in the Rivero events.

Another source reports that during Lieutenant Robert Locway's term there were six English couples, two gauchos, one of whom was Manuel Coronel, and several seamen in Port Luis. This is a total of 21 men, six married women, one single and 13 children, which gives us a grand total of 41 people. Since some people were visitors, the figures tally.

The next superintendent or military commander of the islands was Navy Lieutenant John Tissen who governed from 1839 until 1841.

In 1834 a company had been formed to settle the islands. G.T. Whitington worked diligently in the islands where he had received a concession of 6,400 acres of Vernet's former land. William Langdon, seaman and shepherd, helped him in his endeavour. In 1840, as a result of Whitington's actions, 18 settlers arrived at the islands aboard two ships to reinforce the population.

Eight years had gone by since England took the Malvinas by force, knowing she did not have any right to them or a very dubious one in the best case. But in 1841 England decided to legalize the situation of this illegally obtained possession.

On August 23, 1841, Lord John Rusell, who was Colonial Commissioner of Land and Emigrations sent a memorandum, which we partially transcribe, to the first Lieutenant-Governor of the Malvinas: "Her Majesty in the exercise of her prerogatives cannot provide a substitute either for the legislature nor for the courts of justice without previous approval from Parliament. Consequently, the colony will have to do without any legislature or courts of justice for some time in the future. But immediately after your arrival you have to find the means to administer law and justice within the colony. In a proclamation you'll notify the inhabitants of the Falklands that the law of England is in effect in the islands; you'll make sure this is complied with in any part of the islands where it is possible to find competent people to perform the offices of judges or magistrates."

The letter went on to say that the islands had strategic importance for commercial maritime traffic and to give greater security to British trade.

Doubts and hesitations which only time and experience would eliminate.

The first "Lieutenant Governor" of this unique colony, was 28-years-old, Richard Clement Moody. The date of his appointment was June 23, 1843 and on April 2, 1845 he received the corresponding document with the Crown's seal and the military command of the islands.

In the explorations which Lieutenant Sullivan had carried out on board of the ship "Arrow" it had been determined that Port Williams, (Port Groussac for us) south of Port Luis, offered better natural shelter than Bahia Anunciacion, so Moody during his office received instructions to study the move from one place to the other, and shortly after as a result or his reluctance, he was ordered to do it as soon as possible. This move to the new capital is one of the most important events during Moody's government.

Port Soledad, which later had become Port Luis, the old Spanish Argentine capital of the islands, thus remains only as a very fond memory for us.

Before complying with the order of moving the port, Moody tried to change its name from Port Luis to Port Anson, but the idea did not prosper.

The new English capital, Port Stanley, was named after Lord Edward G. Smith Stanley, Minister of the Colonies.

The capital was moved in 1843 and the governor decided to sell the land surrounding it, while cattle continue to multiply.

In 1845, Samuel Fisher Lafone, a British trader, who lived in

Marine Lt. Col. Don Luis Piedra Buena (1833 - 1883). Pioneer of patriarchs from Southern Patagonia who visited the Malvinas from 1850 onwards.

Montevideo, requested land in Soledad island in the Malvinas, and he was granted 200 leagues south of the isthmus of Choiseul Sound.

The main wealth of the island was cattle and in second place seal hunting, an activity in which sealers of different nationalities, particularly English and North Americans, participated.

There were an estimated 30,000 head of cattle by 1838. This figure had doubled by 1846 and there were 80,000 head by the following year, of which only 400 were domesticated and the rest were wild.

In 1851, Lafone who had a large extension of land devoted to cattle, decided to sell his rights to a London-based company, in exchange for a sizeable amount of shares. From then on "The Falkland Islands Company" became the economic ruler of the islands.

A conflict arose in 1853 between Governor George Rennie and North American seal hunters who were poaching in the islands. The authority of the English governor was confirmed, although it was always difficult to keep the seal hunters under control.

Around that time an American sealer the "Consul Shirley" was visiting the islands and a young Argentine officer, Luis Piedra Buena, was on board.

The colony progressed slowly and by 1863 it had 592 inhabitants.

An Anglican Church mission came to Keppel island and sheltered indians who had been brought from Tierra del Fuego.

In Port Stanley there were Anglicans, Presbyterians and Catholics.

Sheep were brought to the islands and they did very well, acquiring more importance than cattle from 1866. In 1865 there were 26,605 head of sheep.

Second Subperiod (1867—1908). The main characteristic was the boom of wool and its monopoly

Augusto Lasserre, one of our most distinguished naval officers, visited the islands in 1869. He was born in Buenos Aires, and his father was French. He joined Rosas's Navy, and after Caseros continued in the Confederation's Navy. He fought in two battles near Martin Garcia in 1853 and 1859, being wounded in the latter one and as a result promoted to lieutenant colonel.

When the Argentine national authorities disappeared Lasserre retired and arrived in Stanley as representative of the insurance association of the Italian Navy to investigate a naval accident.

Lasserre had visited the Malvinas in 1857 with the sailing vessel "Daniel" and he returned on board the same ship after the voyage we mention here.

During the 1869 trip he was able to stay in the islands for a longer period of time. He travelled there extensively and described his experience in a long letter to his friend Jose Hernandez, author of "Martin Fierro", who had asked him to do so.

Lasserre said that Stanley had between 500 and 600 inhabitants, an excellent bay and then he described the port and how to sail into it, as well as Pembrock Lighthouse.

He also said he had seen Port Luis and described a couple who lived there as formed by a Pampa Indian and an Englishwoman.

He made reference to the authorities of the island, the garrison and a battery with three six-pound guns which dominated the port.

The Malvinas exported penguin oil, cow hides, seal skins, and hybrid and merino wool of very fine quality.

He also described the geography of the islands and its wealth in peat.

Then Lasserre went on saying: "Stanley has two streets only, parallel to the port", refers to the houses, peat storing places, greenhouses behind glass walls, etc. Then he mentioned that the government was not interested in public works, and particularly in improving the port, adding that maybe this was due to the fact that they are concerned about the possibility of having to return the islands to Argentina.

He went on to say "in spite of having a scarce population, there are two very powerful business houses in the village, the Falkland Islands Company and Mr. George Dean's.

He reported that during his short stay he had seen 10 or 12 seriously damaged ships enter Port Stanley all of which were repaired by local craftsmen.

Then he described the slaughtering of penguins to extract the oil, reporting that a gallon of oil is obtained with the fat of eleven birds, and that a crew of 14 men and a foreman after working for a month and a half returned with something between 20,000 and 30,000 gallons of oil.

A detailed description of seal hunting followed and he tells how the Falkland Islands Company and G. Dean's Company were the principal hunters of penguin, seals and sea elephants.

Further on he stated: "Very few Argentines have stayed here after the unfair occupation by the British. There are not more than twenty and all of them are working either as laborers or foremen in the ranches, because in this kind of work they are better than the majority of the foreigners."

Jose Hernandez published in his own newspaper "Rio de la Plata" on the 19th and 20th of November a story introducing Lasserre and transcribing his letter. But then on November 26, in issue N° 92, of the same newspaper he published a longer article under the heading "Malvinas Islands, Serious Issues", where he made the following comments: "The Argentines, particularly, have not been able to forget that the islands are a very important part of the national territory, taken away from us due to very unfavourable circumstances, which the country was going through while still trying to overcome the obstacles which prevented its organization.

"It is easy to explain that very deep feeling which the people have regarding the integrity of their territory and that the usurpation of even a small part of it is felt as if somebody were trying to take away from us part of our flesh."

"Usurpation not only is against civil and political law; it is the violation of natural law."

"Nations need the territory with which they were born to political life in the same way we need fresh air to expand our lungs. To deprive them of part of their territory is like snatching away (from them) a legitimate right, and this injustice entails not only a stripping of property, but also the threat of a new usurpation."

Then he reported historical events and said: "Meanwhile, Argentina has the sacred duty to guard the honor of its name, the integrity of its territory and the interest of the Argentines. Its rights never prescribe."

These words were written by the author of our best epic poem of another period of time but are valid today and will always be.

Augusto Lasserre rejoined our navy later on, rose to the rank of Captain and headed the first expedition of the Division of the South Atlantic which in 1884 built the San Juan de Salvamento lighthouse on the Isla de los Estados and later on founded Ushuaia.

Colonel A.K. D'Arcy arrived in February 1870 as Lieutenant Governor of the islands.

The Duke of Edinburgh visited the islands during the same month. He was the first member of the Royal Family to visit them.

Two ships also sank in Stanley and the crews were taken to Tierra del Fuego on a sailing ship.

By 1871 there were 800 inhabitants on the islands of whom 400 were Anglicans, 250 Presbyterians and 150 Catholics.

The marines built a macadam road in Stanley.

By 1873 Stanley had approximately 1,000 inhabitants, 215 were Catholics, the majority were Anglicans and about a third of the population was Presbyterian.

Carlos Moyano, Lieutenant of the Argentine Navy and governor of Santa Cruz visited the islands in 1883 and returned to the mainland taking with him some very fine sheep.

Piedra Buena had been the first one to take sheep to Santa Cruz from Malvinas and since he had been Moyano's teacher and friend it is probable that he suggested this trip.

It was also Moyano's idea to take some English settlers from the islands to colonize his deserted territory.

Moyano arrived in Stanley with the vessel "Piedra Buena" and there he met Ethel Turner, an 18-year-old girl born in the Malvinas.

Some say he met her during a trip he made in 1884, when he proposed to her and was accepted.

As a result of Moyano's trip several English settlers in the Malvinas decided to move to the territory of Santa Cruz to places such as Rio Gallegos, Coig and San Julian.

These ranchers probably travelled in the "Villarino", an Argentine navy transport ship, which arrived in Santa Cruz on September 12, 1886.

Moyano and his bride Ethel Turner were on board. They were married in Santa Cruz on September 18, 1886, when Moyano already had the rank of Commander.

This is the time when the ports of Santa Cruz, Rio Gallegos and San Julian were actually settled. People with names like Blake, and Munro had already settled there and by 1887 the newly arrived Matheus, MacLean, Fraser, Norman, Paterson, Arnold, Braun, Hope, Scott, Kyle, Jones, etc., were already living there.

Thus, San Julian was founded and Gallegos and Santa Cruz were colonized by people from the Malvinas together with the criollos.

These ranchers did well and formed Argentine families.

These actions started by Piedra Buena (who died in 1883) and continued by Moyano, were the only contacts between Argentina and Malvinas for a long time.

Our position of sovereignty over the islands brought about their isolation, which with a few exceptions, lasted until conversations were started at the United Nations in 1972.

On December 31, 1901, the "Antarctic" with Otto Nordenskjöld and his Swedish expedition arrived at the islands. One of the officers was a young Argentine Lieutenant (J.G.), José Maria Sobral, who wrote in his memoirs about the displeasure he felt to see Argentine islands occupied by British.

By 1901 the population of the Malvinas was 2,043 people and a few years later it increased to 3,000 due to the return of the whalers.

By 1898 there were 807,212 head of sheep, this being the maximum there has ever been there.

The Falkland Islands Company was the principal owner of sheep.

As Lasserre had mentioned the only important private rancher was Mr. G.M. Dean, who had formed a company with his sons; but by 1890 he could no longer continue operations and was also absorbed by the Falkland Islands Company, which became the owner of practically half of the land fit for grazing and of the majority of sheep, also bought the wool from small private ranchers and shipped it abroad. It was a real monopoly.

The other industries which had some importance at the time were whale oil, seal skins and penguin and sea lion oil.

In 1908, 23,774 pounds sterling were collected and 20,369 pounds were spent.

Seventy vessels arrived in the islands in 1866; 47 in 1874, 25 in 1885 and 43 in 1891, 17 of which were steamships.

In 1907, 70 steamships called on Port Stanley, and only 16 sailing ships.

The forces defending the islands during the period 1866—1878 were a Royal Marine unit; after this date there was no one with the exception of the small police force, and later a unit of volunteers was formed which toward 1900 included mounted infantry.

Stanley received an important visitor during 1886, the famous "Great Britain", a sister ship of the "Great Eastern" which was the first steam driven iron ship to cross the Atlantic. The ship arrived in Stanley severely damaged after having hit a bad storm while rounding Cape Horn. It was grounded for many years close to Stanley.

A very important event took place in 1908 when the islands became the centre of operations of a huge maritime empire. But at the time no thought was given to the rights of our country over the region due to historical and geographical reasons.

From V.F. Boyson's book, pages 168 and 169, we literally translated the following:

"This year of 1908 is marked by an extremely important event in the history of the islands. On July 21 the Letters Patent were stamped with the Great Seal, appointing the Governor for the islands of South Georgia, South Orkneys, South Shetlands, South Sandwich, Graham Land peninsula and establishing duties and attributions for governing the Falkland Islands Dependency. This rather vague and inadequate title of Falkland Islands Dependencies includes the land existing between 20° and 50° West longitude to the South of 50° South latitude, and between 50° W. and 80° W. longitude to the South of 58° S latitude. These limits include part of the Antarctic mainland to the South and Southeast of the Cape Horn, numerous islands of the South Seas and also more than a million square miles of the South Sea, easily accesible for whale and seal hunting. The total area is approximately three million square miles or *one and a half percent of the total surface of the globe.*"

The most extraordinary thing about this unprecedented declaration of sovereignty is that it covered an enormous area and it had been done so unscrupulously that it included part of our territories of Tierra del Fuego and Santa Cruz and the Chilean province of Magallanes. The text we have quoted belongs to a corrected version because the original text prepared in 1908, made reference to an area included between meridians 20° W. and 80° W. South of parallel 50° S.

Due to the astonishment and protests presented by Argentina and Chile, the British government corrected the text in 1917 limiting the

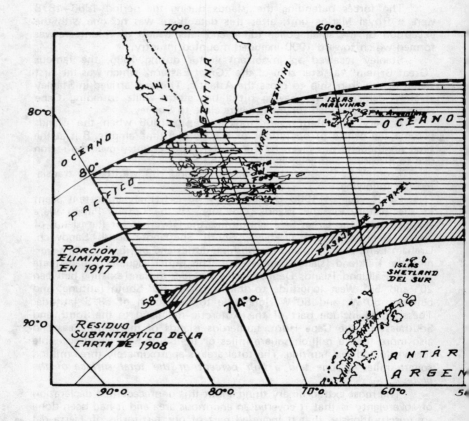

Northern part of the sector which Great Britain was assigned by the Royal Letter patent of July 1908.

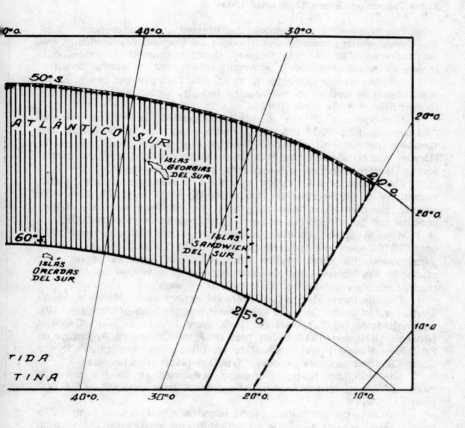

area to what we have quoted from Boyson, leaving out the Malvinas, because they were already occupied and the Argentine and Chilean mainland. Once again force prevailed over law.

Third Subperiod: From 1908 until today

The two world wars shook the isolated and monotonous life of the islands which produced wool bought by England which in turn was the main supplier of manufactured goods consumed in the islands. It was a classical relationship between a colony and the mother country.

Further on we will refer to the South Georgias and South Sandwich islands as well as to the whaling industry which was so important to Port Stanley's life until 1916.

The governor of the islands continued to be William Lamond Allardyce, and by 1901 the islands had a population of more than two thousand people, half of which lived in Port Stanley and the rest in Darwin, and on the ranches. Population was concentrated in the capital and in Darwin, with only a few people living on each ranch.

The "Compañia Argentina" was the first whaling company to start operations in the Georgias on November 16, 1904; by 1909 there were already six companies operating there. As we have seen the British consider the South Georgias as part of the Dependencies since 1908.

Whaling operations were carried out in the Malvinas from 1912 until 1916 when the industry moved to the South Georgias. During these years 769 whales which produced 23,000 barrels of oil were caught in the Malvinas and surrounding seas. Blue whales were the first choice since they yield up to 75 barrels of oil each.

The Southern fur seals were already extinct in the Malvinas, South Shetlands and South Georgias, but now it was the turn of elephant seals. Approximately 26,000 elephant seals were killed in South Georgias between 1910 and 1918. After that date the Compania Argentina de Pesca was the only one licensed to continue with this activity in the South Georgias and they processed 6,000 elephant seals per year.

The Falkland Islands Company continued to be the principal owner of sheep in the islands, where there were more than 600,000 head.

In 1911, the population of the islands reached its peak with 3,278 people. The increase was due to activities connected with the whaling industry. There were 2,360 men and only 905 women. Ten years later when the whaling industry had moved to Grytviken, the population decreased to 2,087 people, divided in 1,182 men and the same amount of women, 905.

During the First World War the British Falkland islanders witnessed two big naval battles. The first one was the Falkland Island or Coronel battle where a fleet of German cruisers defeated the British fleet and then the defeat of the German ships under the command of Count Graf Spee by a powerful English force.

December 8, 1914, is a very significant day and it is still celebrated as the heroic day when all the residents cooperated with the English fleet, either as lookouts or helping with the supply and coaling of the ships.

The islands continued to progress in between the two world wars. The population stopped growing and slowly decreased to approximately 2,000 people.

In 1931, Father Antonio Migone wrote his book "33 years of life in the Malvinas" where we have a thorough account of the islands.

The islands had 2,392 residents, divided thus: 1,213 in Stanley, 362 in Darwin and all the ranches in Lafone. Gran Malvina and other islands in the West had 420 residents. There were 346 others scattered in other places, apart from 51 people visiting. Stanley had 265 houses.

There were 1741 Anglicans, 354 Catholics and 123 Presbyterians, 74 Methodists, 39 belonged to the Church of Scotland and the rest to other religions.

The majority of the inhabitants, that is 2,339, were either Scots or Irish, there were also 18 Chileans, 16 Norwegians, 6 Argentines, 4 Danes, 3 Germans, 2 Swedes and 2 Uruguayans.

There was a governor appointed by the Crown every six years, since the islands were not independent but a colony. The governor was advised by two councils, one the Executive Council, formed by four members, three of whom were Crown officers and the fourth a civilian officer.

The Legislative Council on the other hand, was formed by three official and three non-official members. The non-official members were generally islanders.

The Executive Council was headed by the governor. There were two courts, the Upper Court which was chaired by the governor and formed by a judge and seven people of the island. The other one was the Lower Court to deal with minor matters.

During the Second World War, the damaged English cruiser "Exeter" which together with the cruisers "Ajax" and "Achilles" had fought against the pocket battleship "Graf Spee", in December '39, arrived in the islands.

Due to the presence of German raiders and submarines the islands were protectively fortified. A West York battalion was garrisoned there from 1942, and by 1944, as victory approached, only a detachment of Royal Scots served until the end of the war.

Prime Minister Winston Churchill sent a telegram congratulating the K.E.M. Hospital in Stanley, which constitutes a source of pride for the islanders.

Argentina declared its sovereignty over its continental shelf in 1944 and again in 1946.

England decided to extend its sovereignty over the continental shelf of the Malvinas in view of the increasing importance of offshore oil deposits and fishing resources which exist in our southern seas.

Accordingly, a Royal Order issued on December 21, 1950, stated that sovereignty over the Falkland Islands included the submarine shelf, that is the bottom of the sea and the area adjacent to the coasts of the Falklands.

Technical data was included where it stated that an area of 85,000 square kilometers covered by the islands and the continental shelf were declared British and taken away from our sovereignty.

More than 80 per cent of the imports to the Malvinas came from the British Commonwealth and between 13 and 17 per cent from other countries.

Imports from England amounted to 481,276 pounds sterling, from Argentina £ 21,281; from Chile £ 19,324; from Sweden £ 36,096 and from Uruguay, United States and Finland as well as from the British Commonwealth the volume was much smaller.

Principal exports were:

Wool   557,736 pounds to the United Kingdom
Tallow   1,877 pounds to the United Kingdom
Hides and skins   32,673 pounds to the United Kingdom
Sheep on the hoof 880 pounds (880 head were sent to Chile).

The figures for 1912 are a bit higher, because during that year 5,368 liters of oil and 1,234 sheep were exported to Chile.

In 1953 all of the Malvinas exports were to the United Kingdom, proving that economically the islands were also totally dependent.

After the Second World War the United Nations were formed and Argentina presented there its claim over the islands.

In 1960 the XV General Assembly of the United Nations resolved that there existed a need to decolonize non-self-governing territories.

In 1964 while the islands were under British domain, the Third Subcommittee of the United Nations included our islands among those territories that should be decolonized and on September 18th of the same year the Decolonization Subcommittee accepted that the islands be designated in the future as Falklands but adding the word (Malvinas) in brackets immediately after.

The following year and in fulfilment of the resolutions of the Subcomittee, Argentina invited the United Kingdom to start the negotiations, receiving as a reply that only with the condition that the subject of sovereignty be not included in the agenda.

On November 18, 1965, after the Argentine representative to the

United Nations Bonifacio del Carril made his speech, the General Assembly took a vote on Resolution 2065 (XX) which read as follows: Both parties will be invited to start negotiations to find a peaceful solution to the problem. The general objectives of the United Nations should be kept in mind as well as the interests of the islanders. The resolution received 94 affirmative votes and 14 abstentions.

Fruitless conversations have continued. Argentina wishes to discuss first the issue of sovereignty. The British, aware that the islanders wish to continue being British citizens, want to talk first about communications and exchange between the islands and Argentina, because this is convenient for them and does not commit them at all.

Even though as a result of the Migration Act England makes it difficult for Falkland islanders to become residents in England, the population has been decreasing slowly and gradually.

We should clarify here that all the talks with Englnad about the Malvinas have always included also the dependencies, that is the South Georgias and South Sandwich.

While these conversations have been in progress some Argentine citizens have made incursions to the islands.

Miguel Fitzgerald, an Argentine pilot, flew on a small plane to Malvinas, landed at the race track, left an Argentine flag, a letter protesting British domination and took off again, on September, 1964. That flag is in the Stanley Museum (today Port Argentino).

During the same month a regular airline passenger plane was hijacked by commandoes and forced to land in the Malvinas. There they surrendered to the armed forces of the islands. The Governor of Tierra del Fuego, whose territory includes the Territory of Antarctica and South Atlantic Islands, among which the Malvinas, South Georgias and South Sandwiches are included, was among the passengers of the airplane.

The twin-engine plane of the newspaper "Cronica" with Miguel Fitzgerald once again as pilot, was responsible for the third incursion on November 27, 1968. The owner of the newspaper and a newsman were on board. They had problems in landing because the race track had been blocked and they were forced to land on a road, with the plane suffering extensive damage.

The islands had 628.960 sheep by 1969—1970, and 281.075 belonged to the Falkland Islands Company.

About this time British foreign minister, Michael Stewart, visited Buenos Aires to negotiate.

In 1967 the United Nations voted Resolution 1514 XV which states: Any colonial situation which totally or partially destroys the national unity and the territorial integrity of a country is incompatible with the purposes and objectives stated in the Charter". This was favorable for us and has been used by our representatives later on.

Towards the end of 1969 Lord Chalfont visited the islands and went back to London convinced of two things. First, that Argentina will never change its mind on the issue of sovereignty and second that the Falkland islanders wish to continue being members of a British colony.

Mr. Bonifacio del Carril has very rightly argued that the Falkland islanders cannot determine by themselves what they want to do, because they are actually a factory which has been colonized and exploited by a monopoly which does not permit any freedom to the islanders.

Ambassador Jose Maria Ruda gave three basic reasons explaining why it is not possible to consider the issue of sovereignty as a secondary matter subject to the desires of the present population, and I will make a summary of said reasons taken from the book by Dago Holmberg (page 74):

1) The issue should be dealt with between the two governments and the solution should be found by the two nation-states, not the islanders.

2) The principle of national unity and continental integrity should be applied (Point 6 of Resolution 1514 XVI). The Malvinas were severed from Argentina, which has always protested.

3) That if the British thesis is applied, which is represented by territories occupied by force and populated with people who are part of the usurping power, then an illegitimate position will prevail under the responsibility of the United Nations.

As a result of the Joint Statement on Communications signed in 1971, Argentina had to go to a lot of effort which have brought about the following achievements:

1) The Argentine Air Force built a landing strip with aluminum slabs so that planes could land in the islands. It was inaugurated on November 15, 1972 and L.A.D.E., Lineas Aereas del Estado, flies twice a week using Fokker K 27 s.

2) The Navy Transport Service provides ship service to the islands where they load wool and sheep and return with necessary imported goods.

3) Groups of Malvinas children have visited Argentina.

4) School children of the Malvinas attend our schools.

5) Tourist ships have visited the islands.

6) Norms have been set for postal services and documents as well as some custom duty-exemptions.

7) Gas and liquid gas are sold in a filling station on the island.

8) The sailboat "Fortuna" visited the islands and regattas with sailboats donated by the Argentine Navy were carried out between 14 and 16 of May, 1970.

Regarding tourism, after 5 uneventful trips, the sixth Argentine ship, "Regina Prima", which tried to enter port in the Malvinas on March 2, 1975, could not do so because it was ordered to lower the Argentine flag and hoist the English one.

Meanwhile, offshore oil has become important after the Second World War. Argentina has several sedimentary basins where oil might be found.

Argentina set up a scientific base, "Corbeta Uruguay", in Morrel Island of the South Sandwich Group between the end of 1976 and the beginning of 1978. The British protested and Argentina rejected the protest.

Then in August 1978 Argentina protested the English decision to create a 200-mile maritime jurisdiction zone around the islands, and this decision was never materialized.

Actually in 1908 England had declared its sovereignty all the way to the South Pole.

The ambassadors returned to their posts in 1980.

A Book of Public Records for the Malvinas was created by law N° 22,197 on March 17, 1980.

Foreign Affairs Minister, Nicholas Ridley, announced in the beginning of 1980 that the sovereignty over the Malvinas could be given to Argentina, and that the islands could be kept on a leased basis, for an indetermined period of time. In London it was reported that everything depended on the wishes of the islanders who were not pleased with the suggestion.

The population of the islands continued to decline, by 1974 there were 1,879 people and by 1977, only 1,805, and at present there are 1,800 or less. More than half of these people live in Stanley.

Finally, we should say that so far Argentina has received very little compensation for its efforts in trying to make the Malvinas more Argentine.

The events which take place in the islands affect our country deeply.

Two Argentine teachers live on the islands as well as Argentine Air Force officers and the Argentine Navy representative.

A child born on the islands was registered in Buenos Aires as an Argentine citizen on April 30, 1970.

The Executive Power issued on May 29, 1974, a decree whereby the 10th of June would be celebrated as the Day of the Affirmation of

Argentine rights over the Malvinas and Antarctic Islands and Territory. This particular day was chosen in memory of the date on which the first political and military governor of the islands, Luis Vernet, was appointed, which was June 10, 1829, and coincided with the day in which Port Egmont was taken over, which was the 10th of June, 1771.

The year 1983 will mark a century and a half of British usurpation and it is highly improbable that the British would have abandoned the islands by then. Thus, we will have had the unusual and not very constructive case of a superpower occupying over a long period of time a territory which belongs to a friendly nation without any excuse but the exercise of its power.

We believed Argentina could not be patient for ever, because this would have left us in a position of an impotent country, so therefore it was necessary to change the procedure used thus far.

Finally, on April 2, 1982, the Argentine armed forces could not bear any longer the humiliation of seeing their islands occupied, so they went ahead and occupied them in the course of a military operation where our forces suffered four fatal casualties and two wounded men without inflicting any losses to the British. We believe that this kindness towards the enemy and respect for their lives is a unique case in the world.

CHAPTER VIII

The South Georgias and the Aurora Islands — Their History

Something should be said about these islands since they are very closely related to the history of the Malvinas. England considers them part of the Falkland Islands Dependency, and they are one of the archipelagos under dispute.

The South Georgias are located 800 miles to the east of the Malvinas group; they are 1,250 miles or approximately 2,300 kms. from the Isla de los Estados; but they are twice as far from the Cape of Good Hope in Africa having no geological connection with that continent.

In winter the ice pack does not reach the South Georgias, but surrounds the South Sandwich islands, and there are many more icebergs around the South Georgias and South Sandwich islands than around the Malvinas.

The South Georgias are made up of a very big island, San Pedro, which is 100 miles (185 kms.) long and 20 miles (37 kms.) wide, and some smaller ones. San Pedro has a central mountain range which we call Montes San Telmo but the English call Allardyce mountains, in honor of a Malvinas' governor.

According to some historians these islands were discovered in 1675 by Antonio de la Roche who in spite of having a French name was in English merchant navy captain; but looking at the maps which were drawn later on the latitude given by de la Roche is wrong, because he locates them 10° further north. This is why even a British historian has said that what he probably saw was Beauchesne island, which is about 30 miles south of the Malvinas, so his discovery is a bit uncertain. On the 28th or 29th of June, 1756, the Spanish merchant navy's ship "Leon" discovered the islands.

Until a short time ago we had only the story of Sir Duclos Guyot, one of the passengers on the ship, quoted by Mr. Fitte in his book. Guyot said that on the 29th of June at 7 a.m. they discovered a very large island approximately 20 to 25 leagues long, this figure coincides with the length of the island; then he goes on to say that they spent almost three days exploring it and after they continued their voyage towards the Canary Islands. The latitude mentioned is perfect, 54° and some minutes, and the longitude corresponds to that of the middle of the island.

We've been fortunate enough to find another document in the Navy Museum of Madrid in connection with this discovery. It is the report made by pilot Henrique de Cormer, a native of Saint Malo, and his description agrees exactly with what was stated by Sir Duclos Guyot. It also includes more precise scientific and geographic data which matches with the characteristics of the island.

The island was named San Pedro because June 29th is the feast day of this saint. The pilot tells how on the 28th they saw a land mass, but later the fog covered the area, as it so frequently happens there, so they were not able to confirm that they had actually seen land until the following day.

Americo Vespucio has also been mentioned as the discoverer of the island, but there are many controversies in this regard. Historians are still debating whether he continued towards the southeast or followed the Patagonian coast after leaving Cabo Frio in 1501. The latest documents from Admiral Basilio and Spanish Lieutenant Commander Roberto Barreiro prove that he went on to the southeast.

Vespucio reported that in the middle of a storm he saw a mass of land of approximately 20 leagues, but there is no exact description of its location, the longitude, etc. The latitude he mentioned is acceptable; the land was located between 50° and 52° according to some of the four famous "letteras" of the Vespucian discussion.

The truth is that he just sighted some land in the midst of a storm, was not able to identify it in an acceptable manner, so this discovery is as debatable as that made by La Roche. Oh the contrary, the two available versions of the Spanish sighting coincide in the latitude where the islands are located. But there is a big discrepancy in the longitude, that is the East-West distance, which prompted us to undertake research on the matter. We asked ourselves, why did Duclos Guyot who was aboard the same ship give practically the exact longitude while Henrique Cormer, the pilot from Saint Malo, gave one with a difference of 8 degrees which in that latitude is equivalent to 275 miles.

After checking Duclos Guyot's story it was possible to determine the reason for the discrepancy. It turns out that when Duclos Guyot arrived in the Canary Islands he found out that the had between 8 and 10 degrees difference in the longitude. His work was corrected accordingly and published several years later, whereas the pilot wrote the data when he obtained it without verifying later its accuracy, this explains the error in longitude, the description however coincides. Thus we can say that at least scientifically, the islands were discovered by the Spanish vessel "Leon", on the 28th or 29th of June, 1756.

The great English seaman James Cook rediscovered the islands in 1775, but he admitted that the Spaniards in the "Leon" had seen them before he did and had called the main island San Pedro.

Years later San Pedro island became the centre of the whale hunting industry. In our southern seas we have practically the same whales as the ones that exist in the northern hemisphere. When they were exterminated there, the whale hunters came South and continued with their depredation until they almost wiped them out here. Argentina has not made use of this source of wealth either.

The famous blue whale which is 33 meters long, the equivalent of a third of a block, and weighs 150 tons, the same as 25 elephants or 150 bulls, existed in the South Atlantic and in Antarctica. From one of these whales it is possible to obtain a profit of about 2,500 pounds in oil and byproducts, but for the Japanese who use all the mammal, even the meat for human consumption, a whale represents 10,000 pounds sterling.

The first whaling factory belonged to the Compañia Argentina de Pesca and was established, in accordance with Argentine laws, in Cumberland bay in the island of San Pedro in 1904. Carlos S. Larsen, a great whale hunter and one of the greatest seamen of all times was the manager of the company. Larsen had visited Weddell Sea in 1892 where he found, whales, fossils, etc. He returned later with the Swedish antarctic expedition in 1901 as the commander of the "Antarctic", and our junior officer Sobral participated in this expedition. After the ship sunk and the crew was rescued by the "Uruguay", Larsen decided to stay in Buenos Aires and form the Compañia de Pesca. Thus the first whaling factory was established in the South Georgias, in 1904, with Argentine capitals. The president of the company was Pedro Christophersen, married to an Argentine lady who was the grand-daughter of General Alvear. Ernesto Tornquist, an Argentine, was one of the main shareholders and later became President of the company.

On November 16th, 1904, the Argentine Fishing Company arrived in San Pedro with three vessels, two were sailing ships and one whaler was a steamer. This is a date all of us Argentines should know. The company started hunting whales in December. During their first year, in the first hunting season they caught 195 whales. In 1906 England discovered this important whaling area, and making use of its maritime power forced everyone in the area to pay a duty for whale catching.

By 1908, there were already three factories on the island and a factory ship; more kept on coming, and then until 1930 there were a total of from five to seven factories, one Argentine, two or three Norwegians, one Southafrican and one or two English, depending on the season. The 195 whales hunted during the first year became a total of 95,000.

The British made another unilateral declaration in 1908 when they stated that all the lands and islands existing within a sector limited by meridian 20W and 80W and from latitude 50°S to the pole were under their domain. This sector included not only the South Georgias, South Sandwich and the Malvinas Islands, but also part of Santa Cruz, Tierra del Fuego and the Chilean Province of Magallanes.

It is obvious that the British were not very careful when they established the limits of the expropiated territory and when Argentina and Chile protested, the problem was solved by eliminating from the dependency a small sector between meridians 50° W and 58° W. So this large sector, all the way to the South Pole, is what England has considered part of her territory since 1917. Maybe we did not ask for enough, everybody else did, although using methods which we do not approve, but unfortunately, internationally their policy gives better results.

The Argentine Navy provided logistic and communications support to the Compañia Argentina de Pesca from the moment when they started their operations in Grytviken until two decades later. This is a summary of what they did:

On February 1, 1905, when the Argentines were the only inhabitants of the islands, the transport ship "Guardia Nacional" arrived in Cumberland bay where, in 14 days, it unloaded supplies and 1,000 tons of coal.

The commanding officer of the ship, Lieutenant Alfredo P. Lamas ordered that some kind of protection be built around the bay. The manager of the Compañia Argentina de Pesca, Mr. Karl Larsen, very kindly lent one of his vessels the "Fortuna" to help with the work. Officers Leon Scasso, Pedro Bran, Arturo Sierra, Octavio de la Vega, and Mario Storni participated in the job. The commanding officer described the port as well protected against all winds and with a good anchoring ground.

Cumberland Bay had on its southernmost part a sound which did not have a name, so they called it "Guardia Nacional". The ship sailed on June 30, 1905.

The corvette "Uruguay" a veteran of the southern seas and a very seaworthy ship made several trips to the South Georgias, although the main reasons for these voyages was to change the crews in the Orkneys. The "Uruguay" made the following voyages:

1) In 1909, under the command of Lieutenant Carlos Somoza took the replacement crew to the South Orkneys to relieve the men stationed there and between the 13th and 24th of February, 1909, replaced the men and repaired the facilities in Bahía Moltke (San Pedro island).
   The ship went on to Cumberland Bay where Karl Larsen provided hospitality to the officers and crew. It loaded coal and sailed for Buenos Aires on February 27.

2) 1910. Under the command of Lieutenant Cesar Maranga it took the relief crew to South Orkneys, arriving in Cumberland Bay on February 11. It sailed on February 16th heading for the Rio de la Plata.

3) 1911. Under the command of Lieutenant Guillermo Llosa it took the relief crew to South Orkneys, remaining there from February 17 until May 2. Some cartography was prepared and then they sailed for Buenos Aires.

4) 1915. Under the command of Lieutenant Ignacio Spindola. After changing the crew stationed in the South Orkneys it stayed in Cumberland Bay from February 28 until March 2.

5) 1918. Under the command of Lieutenant Eleazar Videla, it performed the customary relief of the group stationed in the South Orkneys, staying in Cumberland Bay from March 11 until the 16th.

6) 1919. Under the command of Lieutenant Jorge Games it went to the South Orkneys and then stayed in Grytviken from March 6th until the 11th. The commanding officer requested information from the whalers and prepared together with his officers a complete map of San Pedro.

The old corvette needed repairs so the "Guardia Nacional" made two additional trips.

In 1923, under the command of Lieutenant Ricardo Vago, it sailed directly to the South Georgias, arriving in Cumberland Bay on January 29. There they chartered the whaler "Rosita" to take the relief men to the Orkneys. After having done this, it sailed toward the Isla de los Estados on February 22nd. After visiting other ports it arrived in Buenos Aires on March 21st, 1923. The following year, 1924, the "Guardia Nacional" went again to the South Georgias, sailing into Cumberland Bay on March 4, 1924, where it carried out hydrographical work, entrusting once again the job of changing the permanent crew posted in the South Orkneys to the whaler "Rosita". On March 17, it started its return trip.

We should mention that the veteran sailing ship "Tijuca", which dated back to the days of Napoleon III, made trips to the South Georgias during 1926, 1927, 1928, 1931, 1932 and 1933. The ship had been bought by the Compañia de Pesca and in some of these trips officers of our coast guard patrol were on board.

The fact that there were Argentine Navy ships in Grytviken is a proof of Argentina's interest in the islands, in spite of the fact that since 1906 there was an English representative there who became the official representative of said country in 1908.

46.000 whales were hunted in Antarctica in 1948.

In 1934 Japan started to participate in whaling activities. Germany's presence disappeared after the war and their factories were passed to other countries; Russia showed up in 1947 with one of the German factories she received when they were distributed.

With the use of modern methods like sonar and helicopters the whales started to disappear. According to estimates, there are only six hundred or six thousand blue whales left, from the 200,000 which existed. The same situation exists with the other types of whales, like the Rorquals or Finner whales which are almost as big as the blue ones; the humpback whales which are half as big as the blue ones and the piked whales which are between five and ten meters long.

Large whales are so scarce nowadays that the majority of the countries have left the industry, the only powers still active are Russia and Japan. The first one to withdraw was South Africa in 1957, followed by Argentina in 1961, in spite of having been the first one to start operating in the area; then England in 1963; the Netherlands in 1964, and Norway, the big whaling power which hunted about half of all the whales every season in Antarctica, moved out in 1968 but now has started to operate its factory again. So that left the Russians and Japanese. The first ones continue to operate because they are subsidized by the State, because this is an activity which enables them to enter into all the Antarctic area and make oceanographic studies of different kinds, including military, train their crews, etc. and the Japanese because they use every part of the whale, even the meat for human consumption.

About 135 miles (250 kilometers) west of the South Georgia Islands there are some rocky islets, and even if they are small, abrupt, and inaccesible, they have their own history, they belong to Argentina and we should remember them. We are referring to the Cormoran or Black rocks, small peaks difficult to see in this stormy area where visibility is very poor.

The Cormorans are four rocks, the biggest rises 70 meters above the sea.

The Negra rock is ten miles SE of the Cormorans and is only three meters above sea level and, lastly, there is another rock, very close to the east of the Negra Rock which does not rise above sea level.

These islands were sighted for the first time in 1762 by the Spanish merchant ship "Aurora" which was on its way back to Spain from Lima. They have been called Aurora Islands since then.

In 1769 they were sighted again by the merchant navy ship "San Miguel" and in 1774 again by the "Aurora" which had discovered them.

The sailing ship "Pearl" sighted them in 1779, the "Dolores" in 1790 and during this year they were also seen by the "Princesa" of the Spanish Royal Company of Philippines, under the command of Manuel de Oyarvide.

In the beginning of 1794 the corvette "Atrevida" which was part of the famous expedition led by Alejandro Malaspina, left its sister ship "Descubierta" in the Malvinas and went on the check these discoveries. On February 20 they sighted one of the four islands which we call today Cormorans and shortly afterwards they saw the other ones.

They were also able to record that the Negra Rock existed and that there was another rock close to it which does not rise above sea level.

The instruments of the "Atrevida" were used to give the exact location of these rocks. The latitude given was perfect and as regards the longitude it was measured based on a meridian which originated in the astronomical observatory of San Fernando in Cadiz.

The famous whaler James Weddell looked unsuccessfully for these rocks in 1820 and 1822 and so did captains Johnson and Morrell in 1822. The explanation for this might lie in the fact that the longitudes were taken on the basis of the Cadiz meridian and it might be that somebody converted these longitudes taking the Greenwich meridian as basis, without the corresponding clarification, and this was the reason for the unsuccessful searches. Nowadays these rocks have been correctly located and photographed to prove that they exist.

This visit by the "Atrevida" in the last leg of their trip around the world is important, because Malaspina's expedition was an official one which visited all the Spanish possessions in the Americas and the Pacific and Atlantic islands. Actually, it was an official proof of something which we consider belonged to Spain.

The conquest of the Malvinas stopped our natural expansion towards the islands in the South which were already visited by our seal hunters, likewise this visit to the Aurora islands is a testimony that Spain considered these small rocks as part of its domain, and thus they belong to us today because we inherited them from Spain.

Today these rocks don't seem to be very important, they are inaccesible and unproductive, except for the existence of some finned mammals; but in the future, technology can transform them so that they might become the basis for the exploitation and control of our seas.

Our armed forces recovered the South Georgia Islands on April 3, 1982, but they were reoccupied by the British later in the month, after a long struggle and resistance. These islands are ours and we will reoccupy them again.

The Northern islands were discovered by the Russian seaman Admiral Tadeus Bellinghausen with two ships, the "Vostok" and the "Mirny" Lieutenant Miguel Lalarev was the commanding officer of the "Mirny". This expedition went by the Georgias towards the end of 1819, and one of the small islands of the Georgias is called Annenkov in honour of the second officer in command of the "Mirny".

The two ships continued their voyage and found our South Sandwich islands in the beginning of 1820. Nothing else happened until Russian whalers appeared on the scene. But as a result of this discovery the Russians have undeclared but proven claims over our South Sandwich islands, our Shetland Islands, and also over Antarctica, a sector which has not been awarded yet.

Our patience could not last forever and it ended on April 2, 1982, when we recovered the Malvinas, and then the following day the South Georgias.

A hard fight is in process; but even though we are winning, whatever the final result might be, we will never compromise, we will always be ready to recover them, until the islands become ours.

These islands are very important for our future and our sovereignty, and also for the integrity of our territory with all of our archipelagos and that part of the sea which corresponds to us.

CHAPTER IX

The South Sandwich Islands — Their History

The theories postulated by Dr. Alfredo Lotario Wegener as from 1912 in his books "The Origins of the Continents and Oceans" and "The Drifting Continents" seem confirmed through later oceanographic findings.

In the case of the South Sandwich Islands, Wegener's explanations seem very logical and we sum them up as follows:

When the continents, as they are now, drifted apart from what used to be a single continent, South America and the Antarctic were joined by an isthmus. Due to the different density of the land masses, or due to some other geological reason, the isthmus lagged behind and acquired a concave shape towards the West. Finally it fractured and formed an arc, the remains of which are the Isla de los Estados, the Burdwood Bank, the Cormoran and Negra Rocks, the South Georgias, the South Sandwich Islands, the Orkneys and the Shetlands.

At the southern end, the break was the deepest, going down to the semi-solid magma level. This must be the reason why the Sandwich Islands are volcanic: eleven small volcanic islands.

The South Sandwich Islands are the most Eastern of the sub-Antarctic islands and constitute the eastern limit of the Argentine maritime territory.

The archipelago consists of eight main islands and rocks and islets, situated on "a convex arc towards the East, between latitude 56° 14' S. longitude 27° 35' W. and latitude 59° 27' S. and longitude 26°20' W". That is to say, it extends from North to South through 3° 16' of latitude or 196 miles (357 kilometres) and from East to West only 60 miles. The islands are small and their total area is approximately 300 square miles.

The South Sandwich Islands are naturally volcanic. One of them, Zavodovski, has permanent volcanic activity. The others usually show signs of eruption, like the emission of steam and some heat, others are covered by glaciers. They are of difficult access and offer little cover, and it is for this reason that they have remained almost uninhabited until now.

The South Sandwich Islands are located 1,250 miles (a little less than 2,300 kilometres) away from the Isla de los Estados and 430 miles (796 kilometres) from the archipelago of the South Georgias. They are

2,080 miles (3,800 kilometres) from Buenos Aires and 1,219 miles (2,256 kilometres) from the South Pole.

The islands, from North to South, are called:

1) *Zavodovski.* Of circular shape, 3 miles in diameter, with continuous volcanic eruptions. The island is cone shaped and its peak, Mount Curry, is 490 metres high. The volcanic emanations are visible almost a mile away.

2) *Leskov.* Crescent shaped and very small, only about 1,000 metres long by 550 metres wide. Highest point is 185 metres high. Its sides are made up of unclimbable cliffs, more than 50 metres high. There is no volcanic activity.

3) *Visokoi.* Oval in shape, with a major diameter of 4,5 miles and a minor diameter of 3 miles. Its coasts are very sheer. Its highest point is a little more than 900 metres high. Volcanic activity has been observed at some periods but it is mostly covered by glaciers.

These three islands constitute the Marquess of Traverse Group.

4) *Candelarias.* There are two islands: the larger in the East, is 3 miles long and 1.25 miles wide. Its northern part is volcanic. In the south eastern part, there is a glacier from which three peaks emerge (the highest of them being 785 metres high). The coasts are made up of cliffs. The smaller island is 2 miles to the West and is called:

Vindicacion. It is pentagonal and measures more than one mile across. There are no signs of volcanic activity. It is practically inaccessible, and its coasts consist of cliffs. There are several rocks close to the two islands.

5) *Saunders.* Semi-circular in shape, about one mile long. Completely covered in snow. Its highest peak is 810 metres high. There are some signs of volcanic activity. Cordelia Bay is located on the north east side of the island and is an acceptable anchorage point. It is named after the First Lord of the English Admiralty.

6) *Jorge (formerly Montague).* It is largest of the Sandwich group and the furthest East. It is an irregular trapeze in shape, 9 miles long. It consists of a high plateau, its sides consist of cliffs and it is generally covered by ice. Mount Beluida rises to 855 metres. There is no volcanic activity. Phyllis Bay is the only inlet and possible anchorage.

7) *Blanco (formerly Bristol).* Rectangular in shape, 4.5 miles long, 3.5 miles wide. It is totally covered with glaciers and is mountainous, with inaccessible coasts. Danley Peak is 1,100 metres high. There is some volcanic activity.

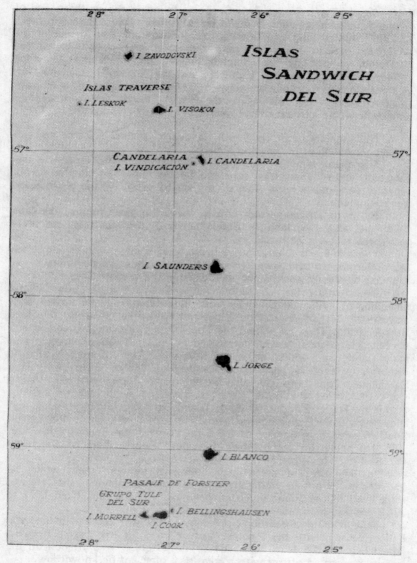

South Sandwich Islands.

8/10) *South Thule Group.* This Group is found in the southern end of the Sandwich arc and is made up of three islands: Bellingshausen, 2,000 metres long with inaccessible coasts; Cook, the largest of the Group, oval in shape, 900 metres long, covered by a thick glacier; Morell, covered by ice, crescent shaped, on which the Argentine Navy Shelter: "Teniente Esquivel" and the Argentine Scientific Station: Corbeta Uruguay are located. There is an acceptable anchorage at Ferguson Bay. Strong south westerly winds and bad weather prevail ninety percent of the time.

The vegetation of the South Sandwich Islands is scarce and primitive, consisting of mosses and lichens.

The fauna consists of penguins, finned mammals, especially leopard seals and some elephant seals and Weddel seals. The most numerous types of penguins are the Adelias, the ringed penguins, the gentoos and the king penguins.

Sea birds are numerous, among them the giant fulmar, the cape dove, the skua, the kelp or dominican gull, the albatross, the snow petrel, the snowy sheath bill, etc.

The climate is windy, foggy, misty and snowy, with strong winds blowing most of the time. In winter the islands are completely surrounded by the ice pack which spreads from the Weddell Sea.

The famous English sailor, James Cook, headed South at the beginning of 1775 and when he reached latitude 60° S. he turned West and on the 31st of January he discovered Blanco Island, which he called Bristol Island. Then he sighted the Thule Group and Jorge Island, which he called Montague, but he considered all these as capes belonging to a larger land mass which he called Sandwich. Then turning North, he discovered Saunders Island and Candelarias Island, which he called Candelmas. That is to say, that except for the three northern islands, Cook discovered the other eight, southern ones, though he did not recognize Thule, Blanco and Jorge Islands as such, rather thinking that they formed part of antarctic lands. He named the whole archipelago South Sandwich in honour of the First Lord of the English Admiralty.

In point of fact, John Montague, Fourth Earl of Sandwich (1718–1792) gave his name to the archipelago, to one of the islands and to the slices of bread with cold cuts between them which he invented so as not to waste any time eating when playing cards. He was First Lord of the Admiralty from 1748 to 1751 and later from 1771 to 1782. He also held other important positions.

The Russian expedition headed by Lieutenant Fabian Gottlieb von Bellingshausen, with the frigates "Vostok" and "Mirny", sailed from St. Petersburg on the 17th June 1819. The Estonian who headed up the expedition was an officer with a great deal of scientific knowledge.

Between the 3rd and the 4th of January 1820, the Russian

expedition discovered three islands, which were named after three officers who formed part of this expedition, namely Leskov, Zavodovski and Torson. Lieutenant Torson participated in a revolution in St. Petersburg, and the island was renamed Visokoi Island, which means High Island.

Some days later they sighted the islands which had been discovered by Cook and in the Thule archipelago he named one of the islands Cook. Another of these islands was named Bellingshausen in 1930, by the British expedition on the Discovery XI. The third one was afterwards named Morrell by Captain Benjamin Morrell who had been to the Sandwich Islands in 1823, that is, three years after the sealer Norfolk, in 1820.

During the 1830 season Captain James Brown, commander of the North American schooner "Pacific" called in at Zavodovski Island, and explorer John Biscoe called in at Zavodovski, Candelaria, Saunders, Jorge and Blanco Islands with the sealers "Tula" and "Lively".

Now we come to the year 1908 and the famous whaler Carl A. Larsen, sailing on the "Ondine" belonging to the Compañía Argentina de Pesca (Argentine Fishing Company), flying our flag, carefully explored the South Sandwich Islands.

We just want to point out that Larsen is the same man who was in charge of the "Antarctic" of the Nordenskjold expedition and who later was the Manager of the Compañia Argentina de Pesca, the first one to settle in San Pedro Island in the South Georgias, in November 1904.

At this point we also want to state how grateful we are to Dr. Ernesto J. Fitte, our recently deceased colleague, who was the first to write a chapter on the Sandwich Islands in his book "The Controversy with Great Britain about the Islands in the South of the Atlantic".

In 1911, the "Deutschland" of Wilhelm Filchner, after calling in at Buenos Aires, headed towards the South Georgias, where it arrived on the 21st of October. On the 1st of November it left Grytviken, but was overcome by a huge storm. On the 4th November the Deutschland's crew sighted Leskov Island and then called in at the other islands. They returned to Husvik in San Pedro, South Georgias, on the 12th November.

Already as from 1905 onwards, whalers called in at the Islands and in 1911/12 Captain Ole Jorgensen called with his ships "Thulla" and "Havforner". The latter sunk in a collision with ice, but the crew was rescued by the "Thulla"

In 1914 the hardy Ernest Shackleton, on the 7th December, sailed between Saunders Island and the Candelarias Group, aboard the "Endurance".

After his formidable feats in the Weddell Sea, where the "Endurance" sank and he managed to have his men rescued, Shackleton returned to the South Georgias on the "Quest" on the 4th of January

1922; but he was already very ill and died soon after arriving. His second in command, Frank Wilds, took charge and sailed from Grytviken on the 18th of January 1922. On the 20th they sighted Zavodovski and sailed all around it, noticing the suphurous smell. Then they headed South, towards the Weddell Sea.

In 1930 the "Discovery II" called in at the Islands under the command of N.M. Carey. This British expedition was followed by a British scientific ship, the "William Scoresby" in 1937/38. Part of its task consisted in marking whales, so as to learn about their habits and migrations.

Other expeditions called in and kept calling in at the Islands, except during the years of the Second World War. The British went there again during 1953/54; the Russians came with whaling ships and scientific ships towards the end of 1957. The North American scientific ship "Elfasyn" discovered a penguin rookery on Zavodovski Island.

On the 6th March 1964, H.M.S. "Protector" arrived at Candelaria Island and some scientists and marines disembarked and stayed there till the 22nd March, carrying out scientific tasks. A helicopter landed on Freezland islet. Plenty of whaling activities took place, close to the islands.

Argentine Activities

After the visit of the "Ondine", with Larsen of the Compañia Argentina de Pesca, and from 1952 onwards, Argentina was represented at the South Sandwich Islands by her Navy, which carried out intensive scientific activities and placed the first beacons and built the first shelter in the Thule Group.

We will discuss the first expedition to the South Sandwich Islands in 1952, carried out within the Antarctic Campaign of 1951/52.

During this Campaign a reconnaissance group was established made up of two frigates, the "Sarandí" under the command of Commander Domingo C. Luis and the "Hércules" under the command of Commander Carlos A. Viñuales.

The objective of this group was to make quick surveys of the islands, to carry out scientific observations, especially biological, volcanological, meteorological and hydrographical and if possible, to establish two beacons.

The Argentine Navy's constant concern was to establish navigational aids. It did so in its sector in the Antarctic with the "First of May" beacon in 1942; in the Georgias, and also in the Sandwich group, although not on this expedition.

Both frigates sailed independently from Ushuaia on the 26th of February 1952, bound for the Marquis of Traverse group of the Sandwich Islands. They had to endure bad weather and on the 28th and

29th of February the sea was between 6 and 9, taking a scale in which a reading of 8 means a raging storm.

On the 28th of February the frigate "Sarandí" suffered damage to her liferaft No. 6 and lost part of her bow, as it was swept away by the sea. As they approached the Sandwich group, cloudiness increased and they met with fogbanks.

The "Sarandí" dropped anchor close to Leskov Island at midday on the 2nd of March 1952. The "Hercules" sighted Zavodovski the same day and almost at the same time.

Both frigates started the reconnaissance of the islands, as previously agreed. They sighted snowy petrels, grey petrels, penguins, cape petrels and Weddell seals and they spotted some icebergs on the radars. The temperature ranged around zero degrees. On the 2nd of March the "Sarandi" sailed around Leskov and Visokoi islands. They established that it was impossible to cast anchor at the former and that due to the high cliffs it was impossible to land on the latter.

Then the frigate headed towards Saunders island and cast anchor at Cordelia Bay at 1300 hours on the 3rd of March 1952. A launch was cast off with a dinhgy in tow, manned by the Commander and some of the officers. It was very difficult to land but four men managed to make it in the dinghy.

As the cliffs meet the waters at a 45° angle, the breakers constituted an almost impassable barrier. The dinghy lost its rudder during this first Argentine landing at the Sandwich Islands. The crew of the dinghy was rescued by a second launch under Lieutenant Commander Jose C.T. Carbone, running serious risks. When the rescue was accomplished Cordelia Bay was surveyed.

On the 4th March the "Sarandi" was sailing close to the East coast of Saunders Island, some three miles away. Because of the high waves, Corporal Signalman Zarate fell and hit his head on deck and lost consciousness. He recovered in the ship's sick bay. That day the sea was very rough, the wind blew at more than 100 kilometres an hour, the barometer was very low, and the storm raged, The volcanic activity on the Island could be seen clearly.

On the 5th March the weather improved and at 0700 the "Sarandi" frigate reached Blanco (Bristol) Island, surveyed it and found it covered by glaciers. No volcanic activity was seen. The Freezland islet was also sighted. It was very steep. On the 7th the "Sarandi" set out to meet up with the other frigate.

Meanwhile the "Hercules" had sighted Zavodovski Island on the 2nd of March 1952, first through radar and then with the naked eye. An iceberg was also sighted.

Then Visokoi was sighted and then the "Hercules" headed for the Candelarias Group, sighting these islands at 0400. At 1200 anchor was cast at Vindicación Island in the East part and the Second in Command,

The 1955/56 Campaign was carried out under the command of Captain Emilio Diaz. The "General San Martin" icebreaker left from Bahía Uruguay in the Orkney Islands on the 10th December 1955 setting out towards Morrell Island in the Thule archipelago. During the journey numerous birds were sighted, among them petrels, cape petrels, whale birds, and also penguins. On the 13th of December 1955, at 1426 anchor was cast at Ferguson Bay on Morrell Island, where a quick survey was carried out, as well as soundings.

At 2020 a launch was sent ashore leaving behind personnel to make the Teniente Esquivel shelter habitable, and to build another beacon which was named Teniente Sahores, in honour of Lieutenant Alejandro Sahores who had died in action during the Revolución Libertadora. This beacon was installed at Newisson Point.

On the 14th December, after the beacon had been put up and the shelter had been made habitable again, Midshipman Ricardo Hermelo disembarked with two civilian radio operators so as to stay behind.

The icebreaker left Ferguson at 1025 on the 14th of December heading for the Orkney Islands.

So three Argentines remained behind in isolation on Morrell island, being the first ones to live there. Midshipman Ricardo Hermelo was the son and grandson of Antarctic explorers. The two radio operators with him were called Manual Ahumada and Juan Villarreal.

The shelter was two metres long by one and a half metres tall. The three of them were living there in a penguin rookery, with penguin dung half a metre thick all around which had a most unpleasant smell.

When personnel from the "General San Martin" icebreaker had gone ashore to make the shelter habitable and prepare it for occupancy, one of the engineers thought he had seen the Abominable Snowman. He told everyone on board once he was back. Everyone kidded him about it saying that the Abominable Snowman was supposed to be dwarflike, very hairy, with a beard and with enormous feet.

Midshipman Ricardo Hermelo and his colleagues forgot all about that story but soon after the radio operators thought they too had sighted the Abominable Snowman. So as apparently he always used to come from the same direction, Midshipman Hermelo mounted guard with an old 1891 Mauser rifle, as this was the only weapon he had. In the afternoon he suddenly saw the Abominable Snowman come out from behind the mist. He was a hairy dwarf and he waddled about. What to do? he asked himself. And he decided to apply the rules and called out three times for him to stop, without being sure whether the Abominable Snowman spoke Spanish. Not getting any reply, he waited for a little while and then. . . shot. And thus ended the life of one of the few pelt seals remaining on the Sandwich Islands.

The adventure did not end there though, as soon after, as all these islands are very volcanic, on the neighbouring Cook Island, they saw a volcano erupt. It was a shattering sight and at Morrell they could smell the sulphurous gasses. The two radio operators set to work on their radios right away, calling for help.

The icebreaker left Piedra Buena Bay on the 8th of January 1956, heading for the Thule Islands and on the 14th Blanco Island (Bristol) was sighted and some of the geologists on board made a helicopter landing on Freezland Islet. Once they returned to the ship, the ice-breaker departed for Morrell, where the three occupants of the shelter were evacuated.

When the trio landed on deck of the "San Martin", they were told to strip off all their clothes and to throw them overboard. It so happened that nobody could stand the smell which impregnated their clothes after having spent one month living among the excrement of the penguins.

This was the first instance when human beings spent such a long time in the solitude of our South Sandwich Islands.

The icebreaker returned to the South Sandwich Islands for the following season 1956/57 under the command of Captain Helvio Guozden. Then at the end of 1957 as a result of a story published in London about the presence of Russian ships in the Zavodovski island which had left a Russian flag there, it was decided to send the Icebreaker there again. The "San Martin" sailed from Piedra Buena Bay for Zavodovski, arriving there on January 25th, 1958. There were no signs that the Russians had landed there, but another beacon was erected and named "Midshipman Lamas" in memory of navy officer Jose Daniel Lamas, who died when the "Fournier" sank in 1949.

The San Martin started its return trip on January 31st arriving in Scotia Bay on February 2nd, 1958.

Our ships visited the South Sandwich Islands in the course of other campaigns, like during the summer of 1969/70, until a decision was made to build a scientific station on the island.

The lava and rock peninsula called Corbeta Uruguay in Morrell island, was the place chosen to set up the "Corbeta Uruguay" scientific station. The construction of this station represented a technical feat and much sacrifice on the part of the Argentine Navy.

During the summer campaign of 1976/77 the two veteran ships of the Antarctic, the icebreaker "General San Martin" and the transport ship "Bahia Aguirre" sailed for Antarctica for their annual campaign with the idea of setting up the "Corbeta Uruguay" scientific station. This name was chosen in memory of the glorious ship which undertook 13 journeys to Antarctica, from 1903 until 1922, a feat unparalleled by any boat of any nationality of those days.

Captain Isidoro Paradelo commanded the Antarctic Navy Group and was in charge of setting up the station, following orders from the Commander in Chief of the Navy.

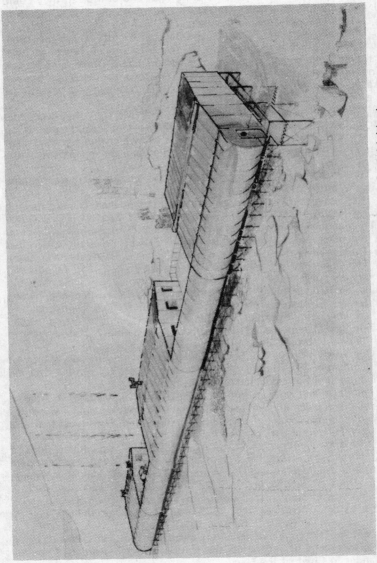

"Corbeta Uruguay" scientific Station, Morrell Island, South Sandwich Islands.

They landed on November 7th, 1976, and after studying the terrain started the construction of the Base, which was entrusted to the Construction Battalion of the Navy.

The ships sailed away and returned several times.

Construction went on for four months in a volcanic soil full of guano, and the men had to overcome problems due to very bad weather and a difficult soil. A large portion of the facilities were finished during this period of time. The very primitive conditions in which the men had to live until the main buildings were finished should also be mentioned. They put up with everything with enthusiasm and unfaltering will power.

The station has three main buildings which are: the main house, the emergency house and the service area in the middle where the generators, boilers, engines, pantry, etc. are located. These three buildings are joined by a semicircular duct which enables people to go from one building to the other without having to go outside where it snows very often. There are also a warehouse, sheds to protect meteorological instruments and a mast for our flag.

The scientific station Corbeta Uruguay was officially inaugurated on March 18, 1977, and a document marking the occasion was written up and signed by Captain Isidoro A. Paradelo, Alberto L. Padilla, commanding officer of the icebreaker "San Martin", Cesar Trombetta, commanding officer of the "Bahia Aguirre" and Lieutenant J.G. Guillermo Escorihuela, Head of the Scientific Station.

Shortly after the station was closed, but it was reopened during the summer season 1977/78 and has stayed open since then.

The station performs a scientific mission gathering information on meteorological conditions, geology, fauna and flora, magnetism, condition of the ice, heliography, etc. This time the Antarctic compaign was headed by Captain Carlos Alberto Barros and Lieutenant Guillermo Escorihuela stayed on as Head of the station together with a group of scientists, one of them being the Air Force representative.

The Navy can feel very proud for having opened this station, it represents an achievement as important as those accomplished on New Year's day in 1902/1919; that of Sobral in Snow Hill during 1901/3; the possession of the South Orkneys on February 22, 1904, and the yearly change of crews which has been carried out by the "Uruguay", the "Guardia Nacional" and other glorious Argentine ships.

All the problems presented by such a bleak, desolate and rugged place which have impressed men like the great English seaman James Cook, were overcome.

There, where the world ends in the "Last Thule" (Tule for us) 1,230 miles from the Isla de los Estados, lies our scientific station, the "Corbeta Uruguay".

The Navy researches, visits and sails with pride all the waters and islands of our territory, even those which seem unsuitable for human habitation.

CONCLUSIONS

The history of the Malvinas which has been so tragic and bitter for Argentina has now taken a new perspective thanks to the courage shown by our men. On April 2, 1982, this country decided to put an end to the frustrations caused by almost a century and a half of submission.

We recovered the islands much to the surprise of the invader, who thought it would continue occupying them as it had done until then.

Our armed forces in a perfect operation occupied the Malvinas and the South Georgias, without causing the enemy a single casualty but suffering the loss of four men and three wounded ones.

The reaction has been excessive and cruel. The powerful adversary displayed all its modern war equipment, but received another suprise, our country which had been underestimated already once, was able to return blow by blow.

Today, there is an impasse in diplomatic negotiations which will end by giving us what is ours, or maybe a bit less. I thik that sooner or later, either during our generation or in the future, this inheritance will be finally ours.

From a strategic point of view the three archipelagos were, are and will continue to be important. But this is not the decisive consideration.

The Malvinas, South Georgias and South Sandwich have economic importance due to their wealth in fish, krill, oil and minerals which exist in the bottom of the sea, all this being a large rich and untapped maritime area which will be exploited in the future. But this isn't the most important consideration either.

The three southern archipelagos are much more than islands for Argentina. They represent the basis of our maritime domain, which today is as large as all of South America and with the application of the new concepts of economic or patrimonial sea, will eventually be all ours.

Grotius'old idea of a' three-mile limit is still prevalent and goes back to the middle of the XVIIth century. This is a convenient idea for the great maritime powers, which have thus been able to take their power to the coasts of the less developed countries. We have seen how England, with it Empire, took over all the strategic points which dominated the sea lanes of the world. But after the Second World War the Conferences of the Sea started giving coastal nations rights over their coasts; these were rights based on maritime patrimony or on exlusive commercial areas and all this has brought about a division of the sea.

In 1958 Geneva extended the territorial limit to 200 miles from the coast, or to whatever distance it was possible to exploit the wealth of the sea. This concept now is obsolete. Definitions have become broader.

Starting in 1947, the South American Pacific countries, that is to say, Chile, Peru and Ecuador, developed the thesis of a 200 mile jurisdiction of patrimonial sea or exclusive economic area, independent of the notion of continental shelf.

The Conference on Law of the Sea which started in Caracas in 1973 and has met again in Geneva and Washington, has mentioned concepts such as domain of the subsoil until continental emersion, that is to say, where the continent emerges from the sea. The concepts and distances involved are larger every day and their acceptance or tolerance has also increased, although they have not yet been unanimously accepted.

In the next fifty years we will see how a good part of the sea or all of it, which covers three fourths of the globe, will be split up in sovereignties either national, binational, multinational or under common exploitation.

By then our three southern archipelagos will have developed their maximum capacity as bases to give us access to the vast economic Argentine sea, which really belongs to Argentina. This will not be possible if we do not keep our archipelagos and thus have an integrated Argentina, even if it implies many sacrifices. This we will achieve without conquering anybody's territory, just by having something which is ours because of vicinity, historic reasons and legal rights.

Argentina's decision is the first one so as to achieve the total independence of Latin America. The subcontinent has fully understood the courage displayed by Argentina in cutting off the chains of opression, whether these be political or econominal. Latin America has also become aware of its potential which lies dormant and which will enable it to become fully developed as an area. It has also understood the role which the great powers want it to play, that of dependence and providing support whenever it be needed.
the role which the great powers want it to play, that of dependence and providing support whenever it be needed.

From now on, after the example set by Argentina, Latin America will wish to remain in the West but not playing a secondary role and not being underestimated by the powers of the West.

Finally, Argentina's behaviour during these events in comparison with that of the oppressor which has been hard, violent and cruel, has shown that a young country has risen in search of a better world where justice, reason and freedom will prevail, giving new hopes to our generation and those to come.

Buenos Aires, May 12th, 1982

LAURIO H. DESTEFANI
Rear Admiral (Retired, in Service)

APPENDIX No. 1

LIST OF THE SPANISH GOVERNORS OF THE MALVINAS WITH THEIR CORRESPONDING DATES OF TENURE OF OFFICE

1. Captain Felipe Ruiz Puente from 2 April 1767 to 23 January 1773.

2. Infantry Captain Domingo Chauri from the permanent Buenos Aires regiment from 23 January 1773 to 5 January 1774.

3. Commander Francisco Gil de Lemos y Taboada from 5 January 1774 to 1 February 1777. This Governor was promoted to Captain on 17 February 1776 and held this rank the last year of his tenure of office.

4. Lieutenant Ramón de Carassa y Souza from 1 February 1777 to 22 November 1779.

5. Lieutenant Salvador de Medina y Juan from 22 November 1779 to 26 February 1781.

6. Commander Jacinto Mariano del Carmen Altolaguirre from 26 February 1781 to 1 April 1783.

7. Captain Fulgencio D. Montemayor from 1 April 1783 to 28 June 1784. This Governor was unaware throughout his tenure of office that he had been promoted to Captain as from 21 December 1782.

   For this reason in some texts he is referred to as Commander.

8. Lieutenant Agustín de Figueroa from 28 June 1784 to 15 May 1785.

9. Commander Ramon de Clairac y Villalonga from 15 May 1785 to 25 May 1786.

10. Leiutenant Pedro de Mesa y Castro from 25 May 1786 to 15 March 1787.

11. Commander Ramon de Clairac y Villalonga from 15 May 1787 to 10 April 1788.

12. Lieutenant Pedro de Mesa y Castro from 10 April 1788 to 15 May 1789.

13. Commander Ramon de Clairac y Villalonga from 16 May 1789 to 30 June 1790. This Governor was promoted to Captain in October 1789; he finished his tenure of office holding this rank.

Lieutenant Commander Jorge A. Castiñeiras Falcón and a group landed ashore. This is the second time that there is evidence of Argentines landing on the South Sandwich Islands.

Also here it was dangerous to land as the launch was badly pushed about by the breakers when trying to beach.

At Vindicación a small monolith was erected in the presence of the Commander of the ship. The crew got back on board totally drenched. Then the "Hercules" headed for Jorge Island (Montague).

On the 4th, the fog made navigation difficult and·at 1400 Jorge Island (Montague) was sighted and surveyed. Towards sundown the "Hercules" headed for the Thule archipelago and an attempt to enter Ferguson Bay at Morrell Island was made but this was impossible due to lack of visibility and also because an iceberg was blocking the entrance to the Bay.

On the 5th Cook and Bellingshausen Islands were surveyed and at 1815 the entry into Ferguson Bay at Morrell Island was achieved. The anchorage was not satisfactory and the waves pushed the "Hercules" too close to the reef.

On the 6th the sea was very rough. It was established that Montague and Saunders Islands were wrongly located on the map.

On the 7th at 0500 Zavodovski was surveyed and at 0700 the two frigates met up, thus concluding their mission. Both ships headed for Puerto Belgrano where they arrived on the 14th of March 1952 at 0030.

We thus see how dangerous navigation is in that area and how risky and difficult it is to land. On the islands the weather is cloudy and the skies are almost always leaden. Fog and icebergs constitute ever present perils for ships.

In the 1954/55 Antarctic Campaign, headed up by Captain Alicio Ogara, the "General San Martin" icebreaker carried out its first campaign, under the command of Lieutenant Luis Tristan de Villalobos.

The "San Martín" carried out an expedition to the South Sandwich Islands and after various calls en route left the General Belgrano Bay in the Weddel Sea on the 18th of January 1955. On the 25th of January it established radar contact with the South Thule Islands and at 1411 it entered Ferguson Bay in Morrell Island, where it dropped anchor.

At 1425 instructions were given to launch a speedboat on which the second commander and a group of men went ashore and set up a small shelter which was named Teniente Esquivel in homage to Lieutenant Horacio Esquivel who was on the "Uruguay" looking out for the Charcot expedition in 1904/05.

A beacon was also put up which was called Gobernación Marítima de Tierra del Fuego. Having accomplished its mission, the "San Martin" set out for the Orkney Islands, arriving at Scotia Bay on the 28th of January 1955.

14. Lieutenant Juan Jose de Elizalde y Ustariz from 30 June 1790 to 1 March 1791.

15. Commander Pedro Pablo Sanguineto from 1 March 1791 to 1 March 1792.

16. Lieutenant Juan Jose de Elizalde y Ustariz from 1 March 1792 to 1 February 1793.

17. Commander Pedro Pablo Sanguineto from 1 February 1793 till the first days of April 1794.

18. Lieutenant José de Aldana y Ortega from the first days of April 1794 to 15 June 1795.

19. Commander Pedro Pablo Sanguineto from 15 June 1795 to 15 March 1796.

20. Lieutenant José de Aldana y Ortega from 15 March 1796 to 20 February 1797. This Governor was promoted to Captain on 27 August 1796 and held this rank until he finished his tenure of office.

21. Lieutenant Luis de Medina y Torres from 20 February 1797 to 17 March 1798.

22. Commander Francisco Xavier de Viana y Alzaibar from 17 March 1798 to the first days of April 1799.

23. Commander Luis de Medina y Torres from the first days of April 1799 to 15 March 1800.

24. Commander Francisco Xavier de Viana y Alzaibar from 15 March 1800 to 31 March 1801.

25. Lieutenant Ramon Fernandez y Villegas from 31 March 1801 to 17 March 1802.

26. Lieutenant Berdardo de Bonavía from 17 March 1802 to late February 1803.

27. Lieutenant Antonio Leal de Ibarra y Oxinando from late February 1803 to 21 March 1804.

28. Commander Bernando de Bonavía from 21 March 1804 to 21 March 1805.

29. Lieutenant Antonio Leal de Ibarra y Oxinando from 21 March 1805 to 20 March 1806.

30. Commander Bernardo de Bonavía from 20 March 1806 to the end of August 1808.

31. Senior private pilot Gerardo Bordas from the end of August 1808 to the end of January 1810.

32. Pilot of the Spanish Royal Navy Pablo Guillén Martinez from the end of January 1810 until 13 February 1811.

All the Governors belonged to the Royal Spanish Navy except Domingo Chauri and the one before last, Gerardo Bordas, who was a senior private pilot, even though shortly after finishing his tenure of office as Governor of the Malvinas he became an Ensign of the Royal Spanish Navy.

APPENDIX No. 2

LIST OF ARGENTINE AUTHORITIES IN THE MALVINAS ISLANDS

Military Commanders

From 6-XI-1820 until the end of April 1821	Marine Colonel David Jewett
From May 1821 or from the beginning of June 1821	Lieutenant Colonel Guillermo Masson
From 2-2-1824 to August 1824	Militia Captain Pablo Areguatí

Political and Military Governors

From 10-VI-1829 to 10-IX-1832	Luis Vernet
From 10-IX-1832 to 30-IX-1832	Major Esteban Jose Francisco Mestivier
From 30-XII-1832 to 3-I-1833	Naval Lieutenant Colonel José María Pinedo
3-I-1833 to 26-VIII-1833	Juan Simón (interim)
3-IV-1982 to . . .	General of Brigade Mario Benjamín Menéndez

APPENDIX No. 3

LIST OF ENGLISH AUTHORITIES IN THE MALVINAS ISLANDS

I — Naval Commanders of Port Egmont

8-I-1766 to January 1767	Captain John Macbride
January 1767 to May 1770	Captain Anthony Hunt
May 1770 to 10-VI-1770	Captain George Farmer
16-IX-1771 to the end of September 1771	Captain John Scott
End of September 1771 to March 1773	Captain John Burr
March 1773 to 20-V-1774	Lieutenant Samuel Wittewrong Clayton

II — Naval Officers Commanding the Malvinas Islands

1834 — 1838	Lieutenant Henry Smith, R.N.
1838 — 1839	Lieutenant Robert Lowcay, R.N.
1839 — 1841	Lieutenant John Tyssen, R.N.

III — Governors and Commanders—in—Chief

1842 — 1848	Lieutenant Richard Clement Moody
1848 — 1855	George Rennie
1855 — 1862	Captain Thomas Edward Laus More
1862 — 1866	Captain G. Mackenzie
1866 — 1870	William Cleaver F. Robinson
1870 — 1876	Colonel George A.K. D'Arcy
1876 — 1878	T.F. Callaghan
15-V-1878 to 20-XII-1878	A. Bailey (interim)
1878 — 1886	T.F. Callaghan

6-IV-1880 to 24-XI-1880	Captain R. C. Packe (interim)
1880 – 1886	Thomas Kerr
3-III-1886 to 16-XII-1886	Arthur Cecil S. Barkley (interim)
1886 – 1889	Thomas Kerr
31-VII-1889 to 19-II-1890	E. P. Brooks (interim)
1890 – 1891	Thomas Kerr
28-III-1891 to 13-IV-1891	F. S. Sanguinetti (interim)
1891 – 1893	Sir Roger Tucker Goldsworthy
13-III-1893 to 14-X-1893	Sir George Merville (interim)
1893 – 1894	Sir Roger Tucker Goldsworthy
18-VII-1894 to 4-XI-1894	T. A. Thompson (interim)
1894 – 1897	Sir Roger Tucker Goldsworthy
27-IV-1897 to 20-X-1897	F. Craigie-Halkett (interim)
1897 – 1902	Sir William Grey-Wilson
I-V-1902 to I-XI-1902	W. Hart - Bennett (interim)
1902 – 1904	Sir William L. Allardyce
24-IV-1907 to 25-IX-1907	H.E.W. Grant (interim)
1907 – 1909	Sir William L. Allardyce
29-XII-1909 to 15-XII-1910	T.A.V. Best (interim)
1910 – 1913	Sir William L. Allardyce
31-VIII-1913 to 30-IV-1914	Captain Quayle Dickson (interim)
1914 – 1915	Sir William L. Allardyce
2-IV-1915 to 14-V-1915	C.F. Condell (interim)
1915 – 1919	Sir Douglas Young
1919 – 1920	St. Johnston (interim)
1920 – 1927	Sir John Middleton
1927 – 1931	Sir Arnold Hodson
1931 – 1935	Sir James O'Grady
1935 – 1941	Sir Herbert Henniker-Heston
1941 – 1946	Sir Allen Cardinall
1946 – 1954	Sir Miles Clifford
1954 – 1957	Sir Raynor Arthur
1957 – 1964	Sir Edwin Arrowsmith
1964 – 1971	Sir Cosmo Haskard
1971 – 1975	Gordon Lewis
1975 – 1976	Neville French

| 1977 — 1980 | James Parker |
| 1980 — 1982 | Richard Masterson Hunt |

Some dates are approximate in the case of English Governors, in which case the day and month are not shown. It is probable that no interim Governor is shown for periods covering some days or even some weeks only.

MAIN BIBLIOGRAPHY

Academia Nacional de la Historia. Catálogo de la Exposición Histórica de las Islas Malvinas, Georgias del Sur y Sandwich del Sur. Buenos Aires, 1976.

Academia Nacional de la Historia. Los derechos argentinos sobre las Islas Malvinas. (Argentine rights on the Malvinas). Buenos Aires, 1964.

Academia Nacional de la Historia. El episodio ocurrido en Puerto Soledad en Malvinas el 26 de Agosto de 1833. (The evento which happened in Port Soledad in Malvinas on August 26, 1833). Buenos Aires, 1967.

Alurralde, Nicanor. El primer descubrimiento de las Islas Malvinas. En Boletín del Centro Naval. (Naval Center Bulletin). Buenos Aires, v. 84, N° 669, oct. dic. 1966, ps. 511—526.

Arce, José. Las Malvinas. 2da. edic. Madrid, 1968.

Barcía Trelles, Camilo. El Problema de las Islas Malvinas. Edic. Nacional. Alcalá de Henares, 1943.

Barreiro Meiro, Roberto. Vespucio y Levillier. Revista General de Marina. (General Journal of the Navy). Octubre 1968. Madrid.

Basílico, Ernesto. La Armada del Obispo de Plasencia y el descubrimiento de Malvinas. Buenos Aires, Instituto de Publicaciones Navales, 1967.

Basílico, Ernesto. Las Malvinas y las Islas Sansón en el islario general de Alonso de Santa Cruz, Boletín del Centro Naval, vol. LXXXIII, N° 664, jul. set. 1965.

Borello, Angel V. Islas Malvinas. Es. 755-777 de Geología Regional Argentina. Córdoba, Armando Flacinga, 1972.

Boyson, V.F. The Falkland Islands with notes on the natural history by Rupert Valentín Clarendon Press. Oxford University, 1924.

Caillet Bois, Ricardo. La Controversia de Nootka Sound y el Río de la Plata. Revista de Humanidades. Volume XX. Buenos Aires, Ed. Coni, 1929, pa. 341-374.

Caillet Bois, Ricardo. Una tierra argentina: Las Islas Malvinas. Buenos Aires. Peuser, 1952. 2da. Edic.

Cichero, Félix Esteban. Las Malvinas: grieta en el mapa argentino. (A crack in the map of Argentina). Buenos Aires, Stilcograft, 1968.

Colección de documentos relativos a la historia de las Malvinas. (Documents connected to the history of the Malvinas). Copilado bajo la dirección de Ricardo Caillet Bois. Buenos Aires, Facultad de Filosofía y Letras, 1961, 2 vol.

Dauss, Federico A. Reseña geográfica de las Islas Malvinas. Buenos Aires, Imprenta de la Universidad, 1955.

Destéfani, Laurio H. La Cuestión de las Malvinas. Capítulo XV de la obra Temas de Historia Marítima Argentina. (The Malvinas Issue: Chapter XV of the book "Different subjects connected to Argentine Maritime History). Buenos Aires, Fundación de Estudios Marítimos, 1970.

Destéfani, Laurio H. El Primer Gobernador Criollo de las Islas Malvinas. La Prensa. Buenos Aires, 1/XI/68.

Destéfani, Laurio H. Jacinto de Altolaguirre. Primer Gobernador Criollo de las Islas Malvinas (1781—1783). Investigaciones y Ensayos N° 14. Academia Nacional de la Historia. Buenos Aires, 1973.

Destéfani, Laurio H. Caza Marítima en nuestras costas, (Marine hunting in our coast), ps. 119 a 152 de la obra "Recursos Oceánicos" (varios autores). Fundación de Estudios Marítimos. Buenos Aires, 1976.

Destéfani, Laurio H. El Descubrimiento de las Islas Malvinas. Aporte para un Estudio Crítico. Ed. Universidad de San Juan Bosco. Andes N° 7/79. Comodoro Rivadavia 1979. 2da. Edic. del Dpto. de Estud. Históricos Navales. Buenos Aires, 1981.

Destéfani, Laurio H. Los Marinos en las Invasiones Inglesas. Ed. del Dpto. de Estud. Históricos Navales. Buenos Aires, 1975.

Destéfani, Laurio H. El Alférez Sobral y la Soberanía Argentina en la Antártida. Instituto de Publicaciones Navales. Buenos Aires 1974. 2da. Edic. EUDEBA. Buenos Aires, 1980.

Destéfani, Laurio H. y Cutter, Donald. Tadeo Haenke y el Final de una Vieja Polémica. Departamento de Estudios Históricos Navales. Buenos Aires, 1968.

Destéfani, Laurio H. Manual de las Islas Malvinas (1500—1982). Edic. Corregidor. Buenos Aires. (En edición).

Corregidor. Buenos Aires (En edición).

Documentos: del Archivo General de la Nación, del Departamento de Estudios Históricos Navales, del Archivo de la Marina Española Dn. Alvaro de Bazán, Viso del Marquez. Ciudad Real, España y del Archivo General de la Armada Argentina. Cartografía de la Mapoteca del Depto. de Estudios Históricos Navales.

Destéfani, Laurio H. La Evacuación Española de las Malvinas. Investigaciones y Ensayos N° 4, ps. 169/291. Buenos Aires, 1968.

Destéfani, Laurio H. Las siete invasiones inglesas. Rev. Historia N° 1/81, ps. 36 a 58. Buenos Aires.

Destéfani, Laurio H. Las Malvinas en la Epoca Hispana (1600—1811), Edic. Corregidor, Buenos Aires, 1981.

Diario de Sesiones de la Honorable Junta de Representantes de la Provincia de Buenos Aires. Sesión del 17 de Diciembre de 1832, Buenos Aires, 1938.

Falkland Island Colonial Report. Her Majesty's Stationary Office, 1954.

Fitte, Ernesto. Crónicas del Atlántico Sur. Ed. Emecé. Buenos Aires, 1974.

Fitte, Ernesto. Cronología Marítima de las Islas Malvinas. Buenos Aires, 1968.

Fitte, Ernesto. La agresión norteamericana a las Islas Malvinas. Buenos Aires, 1966.

Fitte, Ernesto. La Junta de Mayo y su autoridad sobre las Malvinas. Separata de la Revista Historia N° 46/67. Buenos Aires, 1967.

Fitte, Ernesto. Las Malvinas bajo la ocupación británica. Investigaciones y ensayos. Academia Nacional de la Historia. Nos. 6-7. enero-dic. Buenos Aires, 1969.

Fitte, Ernesto. Las Malvinas después de la usurpación. Separata de la Revista Historia N° 48/67. Buenos Aires, 1967.

Frezier M. Ingenieur du Roi. Relation du Voyage de la Mer du Sud aux cotes du Chily et du Perou, París, 1732.

Goebel, Julius. La pugna por las Malvinas; un estudio de la historia legal y diplomática. Trad. por el Servicio de Informaciones Navales. M. de Marina. Buenos Aires, 1950.

Goebel, Julius Ludwig. The struggle for the Falkland Islands; a study in legal and diplomatic history. Yale University press, New Haven, 1927.

Gómez Langenheim A. Elementos para la historia de nuestras Islas Malvinas. 2 tomos. El Ateneo. Buenos Aires, 1939.

Groussac, Paul. Las Islas Malvinas. (Es traducción de la obra Les Isles Malouines. Buenos Aires 1909). Buenos Aires 1936.

Guedes Max Justo. Contribucao a conferencia sobre a historia de cartografía Londres 1969.

Hidalgo Nieto, Manuel. La cuestión de las Malvinas. Consejo de Investigaciones

Científicas. Instituto Gonzalo Fernandez de Oviedo, Madrid, 1947.

Jepper, J.M.A. Ph.D. The metereology of the Falkland Islands and dependencies. 1944–1950. The Falkland Island Dependencies. Londres, 1954.

Melli, Oscar Ricardo. Colonización argentina de las Islas Malvinas. Nuestra Historia. N° 4, año 1969, pág. 195–204, Buenos Aires, 1968.

Morrison Samuel Elliot. The European discovery of America. The Southern Voyage 1492–1616. Oxford University Press, New York, 1974.

Parker Snow, W.A. Two years cruise off Tierra del Fuego, the Falkland Islands, Patagonia and the River Plata, 1857.

Pereyra, Ezequiel F. Las Islas Malvinas. Soberanía Argentina. Antecedentes. Secretaría de Estado de Cultura y Educación. Buenos Aires, 1977.

Ratto, Héctor R. Las actividades marítimas en la Patagonia durante los siglos XVII y XVIII. Ed. Ministerio de Marina. Buenos Aires.

Ratto, Héctor R. La Expedición Malaspina en el Virreinato del Río de la Plata. Buenos Aires, 1936.

Riggi, E. Geología y geografía de las Islas Malvinas. Pág. 41–61 de Soberanía Argentina en el Archipiélago de las Malvinas y en la Antártida. Universidad La Plata, 1961.

Ringuelet, Raúl A. Extracto de la Revista del Museo de la Universidad de la Plata (nueva serie). Tomo VI. Sección Zoología. La Plata, 1955.

Ruiz Guiñazú, Enrique. Proas de España en el Mar Magallánico. Ed. Peuser. Buenos Aires, 1945.

Servicio de Hidrografía Naval. Derrotero Argentino. Parte III. Tomo II. Archipiélago Fueguino, Islas Malvinas, 3ra. Ed., Talleres gráficos, Servicio de Hidrografía Naval. Buenos Aires, 1962.

Strange-Ian. The Falkland Islands. Ed. David 8 Charles Newton Abbot Stackespole Books Harrisburg, England, 1972.

Torre Revello, José. Bibliografía de las Islas Malvinas. Buenos Aires, 1953.

Torre Revello, José. Mapas y Planos referentes al Virreinato del Río de la Plata. Buenos Aires, 1938.

Universidad de Valladolid, España. Varios autores. Seminario de Historia de América. El Tratado de Tordecilla y su Proyección. 2 Vol., Valladolid, 1973.

INDEX